The boiling frog

It is said that if you drop a frog in a pot of boiling water, it will jump out straight away, but if you put it in cool water that is slowly brought to the boil, it won't notice and will die. This is used as a metaphor to illustrate how people don't notice that gradual change is leading to disaster until it is too late. It is bad science but good psychology.

SILENCING DISSENT

How the Australian government is controlling
public opinion and stifling debate

EDITED BY

Clive Hamilton
& Sarah Maddison

ALLEN&UNWIN

Allen & Unwin
83 Alexander Street
Crows Nest NSW 2065
Australia
Phone: (61 2) 8425 0100
Fax: (61 2) 9906 2218
Email: info@allenandunwin.com
Web: www.allenandunwin.com

National Library of Australia
Cataloguing-in-Publication entry:

Hamilton, Clive.
  Silencing dissent: how the Australian government is controlling
  public opinion and stifling debate.

  Bibliography.
  Includes index.
  ISBN 978 174175 101 7.

  1. Censorship – Australia. 2. Academic freedom – Australia.
  3. Freedom of speech – Australia. 4. Freedom of
  information – Australia. 5. Government and the press –
  Australia. 6. Australia – Politics and government – 1996– .
  I. Hamilton, Clive. II. Maddison, Sarah.

  323.440994

Set in 11/14.5 pt Adobe Garamond by Midland Typesetters, Australia
Printed in Australia by McPherson's Printing Group

10 9 8 7 6 5 4 3 2 1

CONTENTS

FOREWORD

Over the past decade Australia has undergone a profound transformation, a kind of conservative-populist counter-revolution.
The Howard Government has abandoned both the quest for
reconciliation and the idea of multiculturalism. It has closed our
borders to all those seeking refuge here by boat, by the use of military force. It has adopted a foreign policy of a more uncritically
pro-American kind than was seen even in the era of Menzies. As
part of that policy, alongside the Americans and the British, it
has drawn Australia into the unlawful invasion of Iraq, which has
predictably seen that country descend into the bloody chaos of
sectarian civil war. It has turned its back on the first stage of the
international fight against global warming, by refusing to sign
the Kyoto Protocol. It has allowed the erosion of vital principles
of our system of government—like the independence of the
public service and the idea of ministerial responsibility.

What has been puzzling about this process is the absence of
powerful scrutiny of the drift of the nation, of a spirited, honest
and intelligent debate. While Australia has been transformed,

large parts of the nation have seemed to be asleep. In a book I edited in 2005, *Do Not Disturb: Is the media failing Australia?*, one possible answer to this puzzle was suggested—the melancholy condition of the mainstream political media. In *Silencing Dissent* an even more alarming answer is provided—namely, that since its election in 1996, the Howard Government and its faithful followers in the parliament and the media have pursued a partly-instinctive and partly-conscious policy of systematically silencing significant political dissent.

It is at the heart of the argument of this book that there has been not one but many different ways in which this single objective has been pursued. Let me list some of the more important outlined here. In parliamentary inquiries government supporters have frequently showered expert witnesses of whom they disapprove with personal abuse. Scientists employed by government-funded agencies have been prohibited from communicating freely with the public on matters as serious as global warming. The independence of statutory authorities has been all but destroyed. The appoint-ment of three of the country's most strident cultural warriors to the Board of the ABC was only the most conspicuous example of the Prime Minister's conduct of a 'long march' through all of the culturally sensitive institutions of society. This process was deepened by a parallel trend—the use of government patronage and the taxation system to silence the voices of the non-government organisations, fully ninety per cent of whom now believe that they risk losing government funding if they freely speak their minds.

The government's obsessive and unhealthy desire for control has extended well beyond suborning previously independent institutions and taming NGOs. When inquiries into catastrophic policy failures are judged to be unavoidable, it has either appointed trusted insiders not likely to embarrass the government (Iraq) or so framed the terms of reference that a politically embarrassing finding can be ruled out in advance (AWB). The same government desire to close down potential sources of dissent has recently affected its relations with the Senate. As soon as the government had the numbers, it made clear that the era of embarrassing independent Senate inquiries was over. Even its willingness to cooperate fully with the invaluable estimates hearings began to unwind. Long before, the desire to silence critical voices at the highest levels of the public service had also been made clear. To teach every public servant a salutary lesson, Admiral David Shackleton (over the children overboard affair) and the head of the federal police Mick Keelty (over Iraq), were openly humiliated for speaking truthfully but out of turn. Under Howard, even behind closed doors, public servants have been obliged to forget earlier lessons about the virtue of fearlessness, and to learn new ones about the importance of not offering unwanted advice. Inside the public service a spirit of stifling conformity and an atmosphere of general intimidation have come to prevail.

The health of a democracy relies on many different things: limited government; strong civil society; the independence of autonomous institutions; the encouragement of dissident opinion, wide-ranging debate. All these values are presently under threat. The Howard Government has become more intolerant of criticism and greedy for control the longer it has been in power.

The evidence presented in this volume offers the most compelling case yet about the increasingly authoritarian trajectory of the political culture during the Howard years. In addition, it offers vital clues about why opposition to the government's counter-revolutionary transformation of the country, in so many different spheres of public life, has thus far proven to be so weak.

For both these reasons *Silencing Dissent* is a timely, disturbing and unnerving book.

Robert Manne, 5 November 2006

EDITORS'
ACKNOWLEDGEMENTS

Our most important debt is to the people who have contributed to this book. In the current political climate these authors and the many others who have told us their stories, both on and off the record, have taken a risk. We thank them for not being afraid to speak out.

Our gratitude goes to our editors at Allen & Unwin, particularly Elizabeth Weiss for supporting this project. We would also like to thank Andrew Macintosh, who commented on the manuscript.

CONTRIBUTORS

Geoffrey Barker is a senior journalist at the *Australian Financial Review*. He writes mainly on defence, foreign affairs and national security policy, but has an ongoing interest in the Australian Public Service.

Helen Ester teaches journalism at Central Queensland University and is completing a doctorate at Griffith University. She worked as a journalist member of the federal parliamentary press gallery between 1976 and 1982.

Harry Evans is Clerk of the Senate. He is the editor or author of several works on constitutional and parliamentary matters.

Clive Hamilton is Executive Director of the Australia Institute, a public interest think tank, and a former academic and public servant.

Ian Lowe (AO FTSE) is Emeritus Professor of science, technology and society at Griffith University and President of the Australian Conservation Foundation.

Andrew Macintosh is Deputy Director of the Australia Institute. He has degrees in economics and law from the University of Sydney and previously practised as an environment and planning lawyer in Melbourne and Sydney.

Stuart Macintyre is Professor of History at the University of Melbourne. In 2007 he took up the chair of Australian studies at Harvard University.

Sarah Maddison is a lecturer in the School of Politics and International Relations at the University of New South Wales, where she teaches and researches in the areas of Australian politics, public policy, Indigenous politics and activism.

Andrew Wilkie is a former Army lieutenant colonel and senior intelligence analyst. He resigned from the Office of National Assessments over the Iraq war in March 2003. He is the author of *Axis of Deceit*.

1

Dissent in Australia

Clive Hamilton and Sarah Maddison

A decade is a long time to be in government. Any government in power for so long will leave an indelible mark on the society it governs, changing the culture, identity, values and direction of the nation. These changes may not be permanent—another change in government can set a different course for the nation, articulating new values that will reshape national identity once more. Yet these changes should not happen without public debate. For those in the community who disagree with government policy, there is some comfort in the knowledge that at the very least they can publicly express their dissenting opinions through the recognised institutions of democracy. This capacity for public debate and dissent ensures that governments must continue to publicly justify their decisions, a hallmark of any democracy.

But what happens when these democratic institutions are themselves eroded by government? What are the costs when a government tries to ensure that its values are the only values heard in public debate? What are the consequences for a nation whose citizenry is denied essential information that would allow them to develop an informed opinion about controversial policies?

In 2004 the editors of this volume collaborated (with Richard Denniss) on the Australia Institute discussion paper, 'Silencing Dissent: Non-government Organisations and Australian Democracy'. The paper documented the experiences of around 300 non-government organisations that expressed strong views about the way in which governments, particularly the Howard Government, subdued their often-critical voices. They reported tactics including bullying, harassment, intimidation, public denigration and the threatened withdrawal of funding. Sometimes these threats came directly from ministers or ministers' offices. The report was grim reading, raising worrying questions about the health of Australian democracy. Although largely ignored by the press, the message in 'Silencing Dissent' spread like wildfire around the NGO community.

This book takes the next step in documenting how the Howard Government has been progressively dismantling the democratic processes that create the capacity for public debate and accommodate dissenting opinion. The book argues that the apparently unconnected phenomena of attacks on non-government organisations, the politicisation of the public service, the stacking of statutory authorities, increasing restrictions on academic freedom and control over universities, the gagging or manipulation of some sections of the media, and the politicisation of the military and intelligence services form a pattern that poses a grave threat to the state of democracy in Australia. The mass of material in this book reflects a systematic strategy by the government to mute opposition to government policy and control public opinion.

The tactics used to silence critics are diverse, including the withdrawal or threat of withdrawal of government funding, threats to destroy the financial viability of dissenting organisations, appointment of party functionaries or friends to key positions, strict interpretation of laws governing release of information, and the targeting of individuals. The methods are often highly personal, with individuals and organisations singled out for intimidation, vilification and slander.

Based on the evidence set out in this book, we take the view that the Howard Government has systematically targeted independent, critical and dissenting voices. We are not suggesting that there is any sort of written strategy or unit designed to coordinate this silencing process. We are arguing that the Howard Government is pervaded by an intolerant and anti-democratic sentiment, one that is at times given an ideological justification, which reflects a belief that it has a right to behave in whatever way it deems appropriate.

Attacks on individuals

Personal attacks have always been part of the rough and tumble of Australian politics, but in recent years there seems to have been a shift in the use of this tactic. Instead of the target being fellow politicians (for whom it comes with the territory), individual citizens have been targeted with the apparent aim of driving them out of the public domain. This tactic seems to have been employed with increasing frequency by members of the Coalition Government in Canberra, often under the protection of parliamentary privilege in order to avoid being sued for defamation. The targets are most likely to be individual experts who are critical of controversial government policy.

Certain members of the government seem to have been allocated an 'attack dog' role. In recent years the job seems to have fallen mainly to Tasmanian Liberal Senator Eric Abetz, who was special minister of state from January 2001 until he was promoted to the ministry in January 2006. Abetz has often been assisted by Queensland Liberal Senator George Brandis. In a range of forums, but most notably in Senate committees, critics of the government have found themselves subject to blistering personal attacks by Abetz, who deploys his staff to uncover aspects of their past that can be used to denigrate them.

This tactic was used by Abetz in an attempt to silence academic experts who were critical of the government's controversial changes to industrial relations laws. In 2005 he referred in the Senate to Professor David Peetz, a professor of industrial relations at Griffith University, as a 'trade union choirboy' who engages in moral equivocation over terrorism. Understandably, Peetz felt compelled to respond to the assault on his character, writing:

> While I am deeply concerned by these attempts to portray me as an extremist and terrorist sympathiser, I will not be dissuaded from speaking on industrial relations matters in public. However, my deeper concern is for the impact that such attempts at character assassination have on discouraging informed debate in Australia today.[1]

Abetz also attempted to tarnish the credibility and independence of another industrial relations expert, Professor Barbara Pocock, then an associate professor at the University of Adelaide, by accusing her of keeping secret her alleged links to the trade union movement. In responding, Pocock exposed the tactic of referring to financial support from one source (in this case trade unions) while failing to mention that she had received more funds from businesses and government. In her defence, incorporated in Hansard, she noted:

> ... Senator Abetz's attempts to malign my reputation were made a short time after I represented, with others, the shared grave concerns of 151 Australian academic experts about the Government's Work Choices Bill ... At that appearance, Hansard records that Senator Murray [Australian Democrats] suggested that questions from Government Senators about sources of funding for my research were 'McCarthyist stuff' ... I hope that it will not affect other researchers, whose work should be considered on its merits, not sullied by factually inaccurate personal attacks made under privilege in our parliaments.[2]

In 2005 Senator Abetz made a detailed submission to the Senate inquiry into government advertising in which he attempted to traduce several witnesses who had appeared to give evidence before the committee. He accused them variously of being 'a partisan', 'a hard-core pro-Labor ideologue', 'not worthy of an undergraduate', of demonstrating 'wilful partisan bias', and of being motivated not by the public interest but 'boosting their own careers and damaging the Howard Government'. For good measure, he accused the Clerk of the Senate of 'culpable ignorance' and of making an 'unsupported, scurrilous, slanderous, and totally false allegation'.

In its report, the Senate Finance and Public Administration Committee, with a majority of non-government senators, expressed grave concerns about Senator Abetz's denigration of witnesses before it.

> ... the Committee is disappointed and perturbed at the personal attacks against other witnesses to the inquiry ... These attacks were unwarranted, often factually wrong, and ran the risk of bringing the Committee process itself into disrepute.[3]

The committee then detailed the factual errors made by Abetz against various witnesses. It noted that Senate inquiries are utterly dependent on the citizens who volunteer their time and energy to prepare submissions and appear to give evidence.

> Quite apart from the abuse of the Committee's processes involved in peddling falsehoods disguised as evidence, the Committee is concerned about whether Senator Abetz's widely publicised attacks on the integrity of witnesses may serve to inhibit ordinary Australians from participating in the Senate's inquiries in future.

The Senate Committee was right to be concerned, for the deterrence of witnesses is precisely the intent of the government's enforcer. Personal vilification of experts who do not share the government's view appears to be part of an overall strategy of silencing critics. No matter how secure a person feels within themselves, being subjected to the sort of personal criticisms in which Abetz specialises is confronting, wounding and hurtful to both the victim and their families. Anyone subjected to such an attack would think twice before criticising the Howard

Government again. In such an environment it takes a personal act of courage to expose oneself in this way. Aware of this, the Senate Committee felt it should counter Abetz's tactic in an attempt to protect the future of public participation in the work of the parliament.

> The Committee records, in the strongest possible terms, its abhorrence of the bullying and personal vilification by Senator Abetz and one of his staff of those who contributed to this Senate inquiry . . . there is no excuse for engaging in personal attacks on witnesses. It is even more reprehensible when conducted by a Minister of the Crown. Such attacks add nothing to the debate, reflect badly on the Cabinet and would seem designed to avoid serious engagement with the issues under scrutiny.[4]

Undeterred, Senator Abetz—who in 2005 declared that 'for some years I have been carefully examining what the government might do to strengthen our democratic system'[5]—has proved willing to launch verbal attacks on organisations as well as individuals. In addition to those one might expect the government to criticise, Abetz has even threatened the RSPCA for campaigning against live sheep exports.[6] As the ALP had a policy of giving exporters five years to improve animal welfare standards in the live export trade, according to Abetz the RSPCA was 'effectively campaigning in favour of the ALP' and against the government. Abetz said he was considering measures to increase the 'accountability' of organisations like the RSPCA, especially whether such organisations should benefit from tax deductibility for donations. Removing tax deductibility would destroy much of the RSPCA's financial base. It would be surprising if this threat did not give the RSPCA pause for thought and perhaps to change its campaigning strategy so that it could not be construed as being in any way critical of the Howard Government.

Another to have experienced the sort of individual vilification practised by Abetz is the High Court jurist, Justice Michael Kirby,[7] but his persecution came at the hands of another government hard-man. The first indication that Justice Kirby was being singled out came in 2002 when 'Howard Government supporters' briefed members of the press gallery on the fact that Kirby and his male partner had been together before homosexuality was legalised in New South Wales in the mid-1980s.[8] The only possible reason for this appalling breach of personal boundaries was to besmirch the reputation of one of Australia's leading jurists, who at times had expressed views at variance with those of the government, in the hope that this would persuade him to retire from the bench. When this failed, the government seemed to decide that more forceful tactics were required.

On 12 March 2002, Senator Bill Heffernan, a farmer from Junee and a close ally of the Prime Minister, gave an incendiary speech in the Senate in which he alleged that Justice Kirby had had sex with rent boys from Sydney and Wollongong and that he had 'regularly trawled for rough trade at the Darlinghurst Wall' using a Commonwealth-provided vehicle.[9] The evidence of this crime, claimed Heffernan, lay in a docket he had received that described the judge being picked up from the basement of the Law Courts and taken home via Darlinghurst, then a later trip where a young male was retrieved from the judge's home and returned to Darlinghurst.

Despite fierce criticism from the opposition, the Prime

Minister stood by Heffernan, claiming that the senator had not abused parliamentary privilege and indicating that he would make his mind up on the issue after the allegations had been investigated. Howard even acknowledged that he had discussed this matter with Heffernan prior to the speech and, in a move clearly intended to add fuel to the scandal, he tabled a letter from Heffernan that suggested Justice Kirby had only avoided prosecution because of a technicality. The Attorney-General, whose role is to defend the judiciary from outside attacks, refused pleas from the legal profession to come to the aid of Justice Kirby.

This affair only came to an end when it was revealed that the documents on which Heffernan based his allegations had been forged. Heffernan was subsequently demoted from his position as Cabinet Secretary, and he apologised to Kirby and the Senate for his actions. Yet the damage had been done to Justice Kirby's reputation and a signal had been sent far and wide that any senior figure who crossed the government could expect to be publicly attacked.

Eroding Australian democracy

The egregious behaviour displayed by Senators Abetz and Heffernan are just two examples of what appears to be a broader government strategy. Over the past ten years the Coalition Government has progressively extended its authority with the apparent intent of stifling dissent and limiting the capacity for citizens to consider alternative points of view. This worrying trend has been observed by people such as the then head of the Human Rights Council of Australia, Eric Sidoti, who expressed his concern that the 'white-anting, and in some cases dismantling, of our key institutions weakens our democracy and may ultimately see more autocratic structures imposed upon us'.[10] Sidoti also observed that it is not really clear whether this strategy is being pursued with a clear intent or is the result of more general tendencies inherent to the Coalition Government.

> What we are really not sure about is whether this emerging authoritarianism is witting or unwitting; whether it has emerged as an unintended consequence of a particular inclination to the way government should operate which is about narrowly defined economic efficiencies and effectiveness; or whether it is actually the desired outcome of a Government so utterly convinced in the correctness of its own view of the world that it prizes the acquisition and exercise of power to impose that worldview above all else and to the exclusion of any alternative worldview.[11]

Australian political scientist James Walter has argued that the trend has primarily been the result of a particular leadership style displayed by Prime Minister John Howard. Walter writes that leaders like Howard, whom he describes as 'the compulsives', tend to be,

> ... hard working ... controlling and moralistic ... given to work and worry, inclined to dominate through moralistic rhetoric, externalising anger and hostility onto selected enemies, prone to rigid world views, refusing compromise or surrender as an admission of weakness, insisting on realism and decisive action.

For these leaders, society must be 'defended against dissent', and to achieve this 'there is ready resort to manipulation'. These leaders might ask, 'if you are in the right, what does it matter what methods are used?'[12]

Readers can judge for themselves whether the erosion of democratic institutions described in this book is the accidental result of a particular leadership style or part of a more insidious attempt to reshape Australian democracy. The underlying message holds true regardless of intent, and speaks to the heart of our understanding of Australian society and democracy: Are we a country that values public participation and debate, or have we instead chosen a path where the only legitimate democratic participation by Australian citizens is through their three-yearly trip to the ballot box?

There is little doubt that some in the government's close cabal of supporters will use their positions of influence in the media to disparage the editors and contributors to this book as hysterical 'Howard haters'. While comment from those who are critical in a genuine effort to further political debate is to be welcomed, it is less valuable when criticism is intended merely to defend a powerful elite. Readers will notice that a handful of names crop up throughout this book: an inner circle of ideological warriors comprised of Andrew Bolt, Paddy McGuinness, Miranda Devine, Janet Albrechtsen and Piers Ackerman, and others such as Imre Salusinszky, Keith Windschuttle, Christopher Pearson and Gerard Henderson. These media commentators are mostly associated with *Quadrant*, a right-wing magazine, and the neo-conservative think tanks the Centre for Independent Studies and the Institute of Public Affairs. Together with talkback radio host Alan Jones they form a sort of syndicate of right-wing commentators who receive favour from the Howard Government not only because they share a similar ideological position but because they are vituperative and unrelenting critics of anything vaguely to the left of a centre that, over the last two decades, has shifted a long way to the right.

As a group, this right-wing syndicate helps to set the climate of public debate, working in 'ideological lockstep' with the government,[13] and often narrowing the terms of the debate itself by pouring scorn on anyone who still dares to articulate views associated with the now unfashionable values of social justice and human rights. As Andrew West has noted, ideological footsoldiers like Ackerman and Bolt,

> . . . may be experienced journalists but they do not consider themselves independent commentators. They consider themselves part of the 'movement' whose duty it is to echo, through (very skilful) populist repackaging, the official line of the current federal government, be it on industrial relations, the Iraq war, or national security laws.

It will be the duty of the syndicate to heap derision on this book, but that prospect has not deterred the editors and contributors. After a decade in power it is entirely appropriate to engage in critical reflection on the effect of any government on the institutions of democracy. The unfortunate reality in Australia is that the traditional keepers of this role—the federal parliamentary opposition—have not excelled in this task. But it is a contribution to democratic practice to continue to demand accountability from governments and this collection makes precisely such a demand. The contention here is that the actions of the Howard Government have put Australian democracy at risk.

An overview

Chapter 2 begins by noting that democracy is a complex and imprecise concept. What is beyond doubt, however, is that there are a number of institutions that are considered essential to democratic practice.[14] These include institutions of government, especially parliament and the public service, as well as institutions that contribute to the free flow of information and provide representation for marginalised groups and interests. Here we might include educational institutions, the media and civil society organisations including NGOs. The institutions that are considered in this book are widely regarded as integral to the democratic process, suggesting that restrictions on their legitimate functioning should be a cause for concern.

Universities, for example, are essential for producing educated, informed and questioning citizens with some capacity to scrutinise government decisions. The academics who staff these institutions require a high level of academic freedom to pursue research that may, at times, challenge a government's values and agenda. As Stuart Macintyre shows in his chapter, for some years there has been growing disquiet in Australian universities about the erosion of academic freedom. This concern was previously documented in a survey of 165 academics in the social sciences in 2001.[15] In the context of growing commercialisation of universities, it found that although direct interference with publication of contentious research results was not widespread, one in six respondents reported that they had been prevented from publishing controversial results. It is fair to assume that, except in rare cases where normal research protocols have been breached, this should never happen. Moreover, four in ten reported that they had experienced discomfort with publishing research that might upset someone and nearly half said they had been reluctant to criticise institutions that provide financial support to their universities. Nearly all respondents expressed a general concern about the state of academic freedom in their universities, with three quarters saying that it was in decline. As one academic wrote:

> The main problem has been the lack of opportunity for publishing results that are not welcome to government and an inability to attract funding for projects that are contentious. Independent, funded, research possibilities are extremely scarce and getting worse with the new emphasis on finding a private sector or government partner.[16]

Since then, the situation has deteriorated with direct political interference by the education minister in the allocation of research funding. Academics have traditionally served as the intellectual conscience and critics of a nation, so these developments are deeply worrying.

A similar process of silencing independent and critical voices has also been taking place among research institutions outside of universities, such as the CSIRO where the government has more direct means of imposing its views. This is documented by Ian Lowe in Chapter 4. The evidence indicates that the role of the CSIRO and other federal science organisations in public debate has shifted sharply from one of openness to one of tight control. An idea of the extent of this shift can be obtained by comparison of two documents. In May 2006 the science writer for *The Australian*, Leigh Dayton, recounted her experience of wanting to interview a scientist from Geoscience Australia, the government body engaged in geological surveys and analysis, about the latest in earthquake monitoring.[17] Her expert contact advised that he was unable to talk without approval from his organisation's media officer. When Dayton contacted the media officer she was told that she would need to put her questions in writing. Dayton uses this to illustrate the 'relentless rise of media management' in which the goal is not to advance communication but to control it in the interests of political masters. Dayton suggests that the gagging of CSIRO climate scientists represents the cranking up of this need to control by 'orders of magnitude'.

The world was very different in 1985. Then the CSIRO's media group developed new guidelines on public comment by its scientists which, in its own words, 'unequivocally encourage staff to talk publicly about their work and to contribute to public debate on issues within their expertise'.[18] In those days, scientists were seen to be reluctant communicators and the CSIRO understood it as its public duty to see its research inform public debate. Progress was being made, with the CSIRO's head of media liaison claiming in internal documents that the organisation had 'become more open and receptive to public scrutiny, even criticism, and we have encouraged our research Divisions to develop their own links with the media and establish other ways of communicating with the community at large'. It is worth remembering this advice as one reads Lowe's chapter. More recently, stung by persistent criticism, the CSIRO has issued new guidelines for public comment that appear to give its staff more freedom to speak in public about their work. Yet the broader clamp-down on independent opinion and the politicisation of senior management will take years to undo, even if the CSIRO was willing to risk alienating a government bent on control.

The methods used by the Howard Government to transform the landscape of non-government organisations are set out in Chapter 5 by the editors. A clear division has emerged between favoured organisations, which receive large sums of federal government money and are represented on various influential public bodies, and those on the outer because they refuse to toe the line. The former, such as the Salvation Army, which saw their 'zero tolerance' approach to substance abuse taken up as government policy to the detriment of the established harm minimisation approach, now exercise disproportionate influence. They also enjoy lucrative government contracts. Certain individuals who lead these tamed organisations are appointed by the government to prestigious positions.

As the chapter argues, NGOs that refuse to genuflect to the government are made to suffer; they are subject to threats of defunding, public attacks and exclusion from consultation processes. An example illustrates the tactics. In July 2006 the *Medical Journal of Australia* published research by three academics at the Australian National University saying that the Free Trade Agreement between the United States and Australia may give foreign companies the right to process blood donated by Australians, and that processing abroad could jeopardise the safety of blood products used in Australian hospitals. The Red Cross Blood Service, which collects all blood in Australia, has a duty to ensure that the integrity of blood products is beyond question, and is the most authoritative source of public information on blood safety. When the ABC's *PM* program ran the story it reported that it had approached the Red Cross Blood Service for comment but was told that 'no one was available for comment because the federal government, which contributes two thirds of its funding, ordered it not to talk to the media'.[19] The Red Cross has come under sustained pressure from the federal government to say nothing in public about blood safety that might contradict the government's position. When it had raised similar concerns three months earlier the credibility of the Red Cross was attacked in the *Daily Telegraph* by Piers Ackerman, who claimed it had caved in to the demands of 'militant homosexuals' in the 1980s, thereby causing many Australian haemophiliacs to contract HIV/AIDS.[20] Ackerman is close to Health Minister Tony Abbott as well as the Prime Minister, both of whom have reputations for being homophobic. It is worth noting that the board of the Red Cross is chaired by Greg Vickery, a lawyer and prominent member of the Queensland Liberal Party (who describes himself as 'high energy, diligent and deeply committed to his clients'). The federal government gag on the Red Cross, almost certainly orchestrated by the Prime Minister's office, has meant that the public is being denied accurate impartial advice about an issue vital to public health.

There is a troubling coda to this story. Not only did the federal government gag the Red Cross from speaking on this issue, but others attempted to silence the Australian National University researchers whose paper appeared in the *Medical Journal of Australia*. Vice-Chancellor Ian Chubb said that he had received several calls suggesting that the university would be unwise to promote the research and that the researchers were 'anti-American'.[21] Chubb is one of the more courageous university heads and went public, branding the attempted censorship 'dangerous', which makes one ask how many other vice-chancellors have acquiesced.

Perhaps most disturbingly, senior staff of NGOs that refuse to buckle have found themselves the subject of personal vilification, including defamatory attacks under parliamentary privilege. Behind the scenes, ministerial staffers provide private briefings to journalists designed to undermine the credibility of the targets. One head of an important NGO who had made public criticisms of a sensitive policy learned that government staffers had spread ugly, and entirely untrue, rumours about his sexual life in the parliamentary press gallery.[22]

It is widely understood that the media, and the press gallery in particular, provide a crucially important contribution to democracy. As Helen Ester points out in Chapter 6, the informed and critical expertise provided by political journalists is essential both for the free flow of information and for keeping citizens informed of the workings of government. Traditionally, a proportion of the information available to journalists has been provided by leaks and other background information from within the public service. Some of this activity is unlawful, some is accepted background briefing. There has been a heavy clamp-down on both under the Coalition Government with unprecedented use of the police to track down offenders and deter would-be whistle-blowers. When combined with the relentless scrutiny of alleged 'bias' in the ABC by members of the government there are doubts about the state of the 'free press' in Australia.

In a related development, in September 2006 the High Court rejected the challenge by *The Australian* to the Treasurer's decision to refuse to disclose documents on bracket creep and the First Home Owners Scheme under the Freedom of Information Act. The Treasurer claimed that the disclosure would be contrary to the public interest. As a result of the decision, provided there is at least one reasonable ground to support the claim that the disclosure would be contrary to the public interest, it will be virtually impossible to obtain politically sensitive documents. The decision is a severe blow to public access to government documents.

Democratic institutions already under the control of government have not escaped the Coalition's constraining tendencies. Geoffrey Barker outlines the seemingly inexorable politicisation of the Australian Public Service, and the demise of the tradition of 'frank and fearless' policy advice from non-partisan officials. The strategy is two-pronged. It weeds out those who are not sufficiently compliant and it rewards those who demonstrate devotion to the government. Perhaps the most striking instance of the latter was the way in which public servants who assisted the re-election of the government in 2001 were rewarded for their loyalty.[23] Jane Halton was second-in-charge to Max Moore-Wilton in the Prime Minister's department when claims were made that asylum seekers in a leaky boat had thrown their children overboard. She was appointed to head the People Smuggling Taskforce. During the crisis the Prime Minister's foreign affairs adviser was an official named Miles Jordana, who had been placed in Howard's office from the Department of Foreign Affairs and Trade. He soon became a Howard favourite. Throughout the crisis, which reached fever pitch in the days leading up to the federal election, these two public servants micro-managed the response of the government, thus helping to ensure that the public did not become aware until after the election that the claims of children being thrown overboard were false. After the election when Halton rang Jordana to tell him that the photos that helped win the election did not in fact show children being thrown overboard, Jordana was 'sanguine', reportedly saying, 'This is not an issue. It had been dealt with'.[24] These two officials were promoted to very senior positions after the government's re-election: Halton was awarded a Public Service Medal and appointed as secretary of the Department of Health and Ageing, and Jordana was promoted to the position of deputy secretary in the Attorney-General's Department in charge of national security and criminal justice.

In his contribution to this book, Andrew Macintosh describes the systematic stacking of statutory authorities with political appointees, the effect of which has been to rob them of their independence. The politicisation of boards and councils can have a marked effect on the capacity of organisations to act effectively in the public interest. When Keith Windschuttle—a long-time critic of 'Marxist influence' within the ABC—was appointed to the board of the public broadcaster in June 2006 he joined two other right-wing Howard favourites, Janet Albrechtsen and Ron Brunton. This occurred within weeks of the removal of the staff representative from the board. Two other members of the syndicate, Gerard Henderson and Paddy McGuinness, insisted that the Windschuttle appointment would make no difference as the board is largely powerless to influence the editorial direction of the ABC.[25] Yet at the first meeting attended by Windschuttle the board decided to prevent the publication of Chris Masters's unauthorised biography of Alan Jones, the Prime Minister's favourite broadcaster, that was due to be published within months by ABC Books.[26]

The stacking of the board and the unrelenting criticism of the ABC by the government has cast a pall over the broadcaster with a subtle but unmistakeable impact on editorial decisions. Producers constantly ask themselves how the government will react to stories and how they can protect themselves from criticism. When one senior ABC journalist was asked why the ABC was not reporting on a certain issue she said it was because they would be targeted by Santo Santoro; the Queensland Liberal senator's role is to monitor the ABC and make waves whenever it carries reports damaging to the government. The desire to please the government can be the only explanation of why one of the right-wing syndicate, Gerard Henderson, is given a prime spot on Radio National's *Breakfast* program, in which he is presented as an independent commentator. Henderson, who once served as the Prime Minister's chief of staff, takes the opportunity to defend John Howard and attack the opposition.

The Australia Council is another cultural institution that has been targeted by the Howard Government for failing to toe the line. In 2005, the council helped fund a play by well-known playwright Hannie Rayson titled *Two Brothers*. Based on the relationship between Peter and Tim Costello, the play concerned the treatment of asylum seekers and painted an unflattering picture of the Treasurer. When the play ran in Sydney and Melbourne it was attacked by Andrew Bolt in the *Herald-Sun* as a 'vomit of smug hate', and so outraged was the government that senior ministers discussed abolishing the Australia Council.[27] Arts Minister Rod Kemp is reported to have said to the chair of the Melbourne Theatre Company, 'Why do you persist in biting the hand that feeds?' In June 2006 the government announced that it had appointed Imre Salusinszky, a Howard Government darling once touted as the 'right-wing Phillip Adams', to chair the Australia Council Literature Board. An unmistakeable message has been sent to Australia's premier arts funding body: if you fund critics of the government the money will dry up.

In the final chapter of the book, Clerk of the Senate Harry Evans describes the diminishing capacity of the Senate to scrutinise government decisions and fulfil its role as one of the checks on executive power. Despite Prime Minister Howard's promise that his government would use its newly acquired control of the Senate responsibly, the opposite has proved to be the case. The silencing mechanisms of the gag and the guillotine have been imposed with alarming frequency, most disturbingly during debates on the most controversial pieces of legislation. Despite the Prime Minister's 2006 claim that his is 'the most accountable executive since federation', the government's further restrictions on the Senate committee system—which sharply reduced the number of committees and ensured that each would be chaired and controlled by the government—in fact suggest a government determined to reduce public scrutiny of its decisions and diminish its own accountability. We can no longer expect a government enforcer such as Eric Abetz to be disciplined by the Senate or its committees for his personal attacks on witnesses, as all committees are now firmly supervised by the government.

In sum, the chapters in this book paint a picture of Australian democracy in serious jeopardy. Over the last few years many people have wondered aloud how it is that the government, and especially the Prime Minister, have escaped censure for creating a culture of political deception. We believe that the transformation of the democratic landscape as described in this book explains how and why the government has not been brought to account. Beyond the limited democracy offered by the electoral process, there is now much tighter control over the flow of information that should help to keep citizens informed, there are fewer forums in which dissenting voices can be heard, and there is an increasingly rigid insistence that only those anointed by the government should be heard at all. The longer term picture is even more worrying: authoritarianism can only flourish where democracy has been eroded. If you think that is alarmist, read on!

2
Redefining democracy

Sarah Maddison

Australia did not begin as a democracy. Britain was a constitutional monarchy when it colonised this country, and for the first 50 years of the European presence here the colonial governors ruled autocratically. There was no such thing as parliaments or citizens, and the types of democratic freedoms that we take for granted today had yet to be imagined.

Gradually over time, things changed. When the transportation of convicts ended there was progress in the evolution of Australian self-government towards a representative system of responsible government. In fact, Australia became 'devoted to democracy' at a time when many European nations were neglecting or even rejecting democratic notions.[1] The democratic innovations that developed here—including universal suffrage, the secret ballot and compulsory voting—came at a great price to the Indigenous nations (with their own distinctive forms of governance) that had existed here for thousands of years prior to the arrival of the Europeans, yet as a remote colonial outpost Australia was seen by many

to offer the opportunity for democratic progress and even experi-
mentation 'without the fetters of entrenched aristocratic rule'.[2]

In many ways Australian democracy remains a work in
progress. Democracy is never fixed or static, nor is it restricted to
theoretical discussion in textbooks. There are various models of
democracy that continue to change and evolve through political
practice, including public debate and the reform of institutions.
The etymological origins of the word itself immediately suggest
the unfixed nature of the concept. Derived from two Greek
words—'demos', which means people, and 'kratos', which means
rule—we arrive at the most common understanding of democracy, that is, 'rule by the people'. But who are the people? And
how should they rule? These questions form the basis of this
chapter, which in turn informs the view of democracy that under-
pins this book.

What is democracy?

Democracy remains, as Winston Churchill once observed, the
'least worst' form of government. Australian democracy is
arguably better than most; we are clearly better off than many
countries that do not experience our level of democratic freedoms.
But we should not allow ourselves to become complacent in this
regard. Our style of representative, liberal democracy may be the
dominant form of western-style government, but as Graham
Maddox, one of Australia's foremost political scientists points out,
'we should not be too confident in accepting [the] permanence, or
even [the] virtue' of our system of democracy as compared with
other systems.[3]

Democracy is still a relatively recent phenomenon. Its development is linked to other changes in Western societies, including the gradual weakening of monarchies as acceptable systems of governance, the development of industrialisation and capitalism and the rise in private ownership of property—one of the earlier conditions required for the granting of suffrage. But as to what actually defines democracy, there can be no simple answer. There are many models and much complex democracy theory, and this is not the place to provide a review of that work. However, it is important for the framework of this book to acknowledge that democracy is what is known as an 'essentially contested concept'—it is an idea about which there can be no single definition and about which people can legitimately hold quite different meanings.[4]

Despite this conceptual complexity there is agreement about what constitute the essential elements of democratic governance. The practice of democracy is generally understood as comprising a number of different institutions including parliament, the justice system and the executive, which governs the bureaucracy. These interlocking institutions are intended to operate independently of one another under the doctrine of the separation of powers. Democratic governance also includes certain key social and cultural institutions and practices such as the media, education systems and civil society, which can enhance the capacity for citizens to engage in debate and protest. Democracy in this sense is considered to have a number of in-built 'checks and balances' to ensure the accountability and integrity of elected officials through the public scrutiny of their activities. As Maddox argues: 'The state cannot be democratic unless it rests upon a "democratic" society. But the society cannot be democratic except it be protected by a state which, although necessarily "oligarchic" in form, is run on democratic principles.'[5]

But if democracy is so complicated and difficult to understand how can this book make a claim that the Coalition Government is eroding Australian democracy? Surely it is more feasible to suggest that the Prime Minister and the Coalition Government merely have a view of democracy that differs greatly from that of the contributors to this book. Just because Howard's view of democracy differs from the view that animates those concerned with concepts such as social justice and human rights doesn't make it any less democratic, does it?

We believe that it does. To suggest that democracy is complicated and open to different interpretations is not to concede that it is not possible to measure the health of democracy in any particular polity. Various international efforts are underway to do just that, led by the work of the International Institute for Democracy and Electoral Assistance (IDEA), based in Sweden. IDEA has developed various tools for 'auditing' democracy, found in their *Handbook for Democracy Assessment*, and have published the findings of assessments done in Bangladesh, El Salvador, Italy, Kenya, South Korea, Malawi, New Zealand and Peru.[6] Here, the Democratic Audit of Australia has been funded by the Australian Research Council and is led by Professor Marian Sawer at the Australian National University in Canberra.

The work of these groups in assessing democracy is guided by some core values. Central to these are the ideas of popular control over public decision-making and the necessity of political equality in exercising that control (to ensure that popular majorities do not override respect for a diversity of minority voices). In addition, the Australian audit team also adopted the principles of human rights and civil liberties, and stressed the importance of the quality of public debate as guiding values for their work.[7]

The various attempts to measure the quality of democracy all stress its complexity and internal contradictions. However, there are a number of key features that are consistently examined, including the constitutional limitation of government powers, the importance of a 'responsible' executive, the necessity for a vigorous opposition and an overall commitment to practices that are inclusive, participatory, representative, accountable, transparent and responsive to citizens' aspirations and expectations.[8] What is common to these attempts to measure democracy is an emphasis on the capacity for some degree of citizen control that goes beyond the ballot box and extends to genuine participatory practices. Democracy is not just voting, it includes a capacity for civics or citizenship activities, participation in public life and the ability of citizens to have some meaningful influence over the shape and role of social and political institutions. In other words, democracy is about the activities and capacities of citizens, not just governments.[9]

Participation and civic engagement are thought important for good democracy for a number of reasons. First, this type of engagement improves the quality of democratic governance by providing governments with knowledge of the interests of the people. Second, governments and the decisions that they make can be seen to be truly legitimate only when a wide diversity of 'the people' are mobilised and participate in their self-rule. Third, participation itself can enhance the quality of people's lives because it involves the exercise of distinctive human capacities and can be considered an intrinsically noble enterprise.[10]

Governments can respond to this demand for greater citizen participation in many ways. They have a choice in the way they relate to democratic institutions that can be best understood by a single metaphor: democratic governance can be conceived of as a pair of arms around a society's democratic institutions. These arms can either embrace and support those institutions or they can constrain their capacity to contribute to democratic participation.[11] Governments committed to a continuing process of democratisation enhance the authenticity of popular control, encouraging and enabling citizen participation in order to make this control real rather than symbolic.[12] Governments that are threatened by participation, particularly by those with whom they disagree, are less likely to embrace the mobilisation of groups representing interests at odds with their own, and may take steps to ensure that the institutions and practices that would contribute to those people being informed and enabled to mobilise are controlled by the government itself.

Political theorists Hugh Emy and Owen Hughes have noted that often these embracing or constraining tendencies are aligned with a position on the ideological spectrum of liberalism. They note that,

> . . . as one moves from the intellectual Left of liberalism Right-wards across its centre, the greater is the tendency to conceptualise democracy in procedural terms, to adopt a minimalist definition of it . . . The further Left-wards one travels across the political spectrum the more strongly the values and principles of 'democracy' are accepted as an alternative way of organising social (and productive) life.[13]

The central argument of this book is that during the past decade, the Coalition Government in Australia has applied its ideologically influenced, minimalist conception of democracy to Australian political practice with deleterious effects on our political, governmental and social institutions. This process has been complicated and exacerbated by the concurrent trends of neo-liberalism in public sector management. Rather than attempting to ameliorate the inevitable deficit in Australian representative democracy,[14] recent years have seen a dangerous erosion of our democratic institutions.[15]

What's wrong with Australian democracy?

A number of problems in Australian democracy have become increasingly evident since the election of the Coalition in 1996. At first glance, the initial problem may appear to have little to do with the Coalition Government itself. As has been noted above, a vigorous parliamentary opposition is important to democracy as it should ensure that a government is 'questioned, challenged, probed and opposed' in a manner that helps keep it accountable to the people.[16] The federal Australian Labor Party (ALP) has not been such an opposition. This is not the place to detail the woes of the ALP, except to note that its internal politics, poor parliamentary performance and leadership, and lack of policy activism have done little to challenge, probe or scrutinise Coalition Government decisions.[17]

But this book is not about the ALP. Our concern here is with the Coalition Government's response to this situation. A more responsible government, with a greater commitment to democracy rather than power, would see the need to enhance rather than diminish opportunities for public scrutiny of its decisions.

In eroding and constraining Australia's democratic institutions Prime Minister Howard and the Coalition are following in a tradition of what is known as 'revisionist democracy'. In this view it is wrong to envisage an actively engaged citizenry participating in a diversity of democratic processes and holding the government of the day accountable, other than at election time. The role of the citizen is restricted to voting, and the apathy and ignorance of the average citizen is emphasised. Above all, discussion, debate and dissent are to be kept to a minimum, as exemplified in the views of one of its North American exponents, Harold Lasswell:

> Discussion frequently complicates social difficulties, for the discussion of far-flung interests arouses a psychology of conflict which produces obstructive, fictitious and irrelevant values. The problem of politics is less to solve conflicts than to prevent them; less to serve as a safety valve for social protest than to apply social energy to the abolition of recurrent sources of strain in society.[18]

This view is echoed strongly in John Howard's oft-stated commitment of governing for the Australian 'mainstream'.[19] In his view, those who would challenge or criticise government policy are a 'noisy minority'. His aim is for Australians to feel 'relaxed and comfortable', a state that includes political disengagement. Indeed, he has said that politics should 'not stir the passions of the people, and should be kept off the front pages of the newspapers'.[20] Applied to the media, to universities and to the NGO sector, this view has overseen a decline in the range of views to be heard in public debates. The references to 'mainstream Australia' and 'political correctness' and the dismissal of critics as 'out-of-touch elites' have dramatically reduced the range of legitimate voices in public debates.

At a deeper level, the revisionist view of democracy advanced by the Howard Government rests upon a particular belief about human nature. This view considers that it is normal and natural for people to be the self-interested 'rational maximisers' known as *homo economicus* in the economics textbooks. In this view human beings are understood to be 'fundamentally acquisitive creatures' for whom 'consumption and acquisition are the means to happiness'.[21] The purpose of society, then, is 'to provide the secure space in which these naturally self-interested individuals are left free to discover and pursue their own (basically material) happiness'.[22] This is hardly a modern view; the idea of government as being structured around the self-interested individual dates back to Hobbes and Locke. In the modern variation—known as rational choice theory, and its offspring, public choice theory—citizens are regarded as having little concern with democratic participation unless it is in their own material interests. In turn the model of government designed to support the activities of the 'instrumentally rational egoist' is a 'minimal democracy' that can at best provide 'few safeguards against tyranny'.[23]

A wholly different view of human nature sees human beings as creatures with 'unique capacities for leading rational and moral lives'.[24] The capacities to reason and moralise are seen to equip people with the ability to make judgements and determine right from wrong. Such a view animates a more embracing government relationship with democratic institutions for it places faith in the power of judgement of the citizenry.[25] In our view, the Howard Government has shown that it lacks this faith.

Why does it matter?

Australia, like other Western liberal democracies, is showing evidence of both declining confidence and declining participation by citizens in democratic processes. The pre-eminence of *homo economicus* in neo-liberal economic and political theory has acted as a self-fulfilling prophecy that has promoted self-interest as a virtue. This has arguably contributed to electoral outcomes driven by fear (of terrorism and an 'invasion' of asylum seekers, as in 2001) and greed (in the 'interest-rate election' of 2004). Citizens see little value or virtue in political engagement or participation beyond their own interests, although they do continue to make a distinction between their support for democracy as an ideal and their disengagement from, and distrust in, the institutional forms of Australian parliamentary democracy.[26] This disengagement is further exacerbated by restrictions on the flow of information to the public. The silencing of critical voices in the university and research sectors and in the media, for example, has a direct impact on the average Australian citizen's capacity to be informed and therefore to participate.

This disengagement has worrying implications. An extensive study of political disengagement in the United Kingdom concluded that, among other problems, disengagement created a climate in which a 'quiet authoritarianism' can flourish.[27] By this, the study's authors meant a situation could develop where governments are, effectively, no longer held to account and where policy and law are made 'in consultation with a small coterie of support-ers and with little reference to wider views and interests'. They argue that in such circumstances, other democratic processes and institutions, including elections, become 'empty rituals'. The silencing of dissenting and independent opinion in the various institutions described in this book is a decisive move towards this form of authoritarianism.

It can certainly be argued that those who are most determined to suppress dissent and controversy are most likely to be those who will gain from this suppression. Politicians may exercise power in ways they could not defend if they were required to justify it 'in the light of public debate'.[28] As a revisionist democrat, it is unsurprising that a leader such as Howard would pursue a silencing strategy. But these strategies are dangerous for democ-racy. As the political scientist James Walter has argued, a leader such as Howard, whose,

> . . . own proclivities enhance the funnelling effect of more centralisation, tight inner circles, closed systems and personal policy control may be especially prone to risky decisions . . . Conscious of such outcomes as being inherently vulnerable to scrutiny, the inner circle will then resort to ethically dubious measures to control information . . .[29]

There are important reasons to value a more open and participatory form of democratic practice that encourages debate and does not shy away from or suppress dissent. Many benefits accrue to governments that choose the democratic embrace. They may find themselves in a stronger position to explain and justify their decisions and may also find themselves holding stronger 'democratic credentials', both at home and on the international stage.[30] Democratic accountability is enhanced in an environment where political decisions are seen as needing input from a wide range of contributors who may be affected by these decisions. Embracing governments can show themselves to be 'open and trustworthy', thus enhancing the legitimacy of government in general and thereby creating a stronger democracy.[31] And democratic participation and debate produces better policy decisions because individuals are protected from the possibly damaging effects of decisions taken without their knowledge, and because the activity of participation itself is an educational experience.[32]

Prime Minister Howard himself has made an argument for the importance of debate, at least in his own party room. Writing of the federal parliamentary Liberal Party, he argues that:

> Whether it's further economic reform, or social reform, or constitutional reform none of us should be frightened of engaging in a constructive debate . . . We will not always agree on what to do or how we should do it. But with goodwill on all sides we can work our way through difficult issues.[33]

The same goodwill is not extended to those outside of the party room. As Australia's democratic credentials are eroded there is much reason to be concerned. As political scientist Lyn Carson has suggested, the solution to political disengagement and dissatisfaction is not less democracy, it is '*deeper* democracy'.[34]

The disengagement observed here and elsewhere is not just a concern with the so-called 'chattering classes' or 'chardonnay socialists'—although some in the government would have us believe that such preoccupations are merely the exaggerated concern of such out-of-touch 'elites'. Revitalising the institutions of democracy is a project that will do much to alleviate the cynicism, depression and anger that result from this minimalist, revisionist democracy that denies Australians their capacities as engaged citizens concerned with more than merely their own self-interest. But these problems will not fix themselves. It will take both political action and citizen awareness, concern and participation to rebuild the institutions of Australian democracy.

This project should be a priority. As Maddox argues:

> If we truly value the freedom that our leaders say we do . . . we shall uphold our democracy even against those very same leaders. The alternatives are too horrible to contemplate, for anything less threatens the loss of our freedom and autonomy . . .[35]

The nature of democracy, and the values discussed above, suggest that defence of democratic freedom should be the business of everybody. We cannot take the survival of democratic values and practice for granted, especially in the face of a creeping authoritarianism.

What kind of democracy do we want?

The Howard Government believes in a revisionist, minimalist version of democracy that cares little for genuine public participation or deliberation and that seeks to silence dissenting and independent opinion wherever possible. The following chapters in this book detail the effects of this constraining democracy on the most important democratic institutions. This can be contrasted with a more participatory, deliberative, embracing democracy that values dissent and debate, and that conceives of its citizens as capable and concerned to engage in political practice.

It is almost universally true that the practice of modern democratic politics occurs under representative systems of government. These systems are acknowledged to create few opportunities for ordinary citizens to exercise genuine influence.[36] This situation is one that demands of governments the responsibility to maximise rather than minimise such opportunities where they occur. Citizens may participate formally or informally via submissions to parliamentary inquiries, letters to the editor, volunteering at an NGO or even, through debate and discussion among friends and colleagues, by deliberating upon political events and making the effort to be informed and engaged. One effect of revisionist democracy is the 'dumbing down' of citizens; one response is to demand information and the public justification of political decisions.

Public justification is important because it is not adequate for political leaders, who may claim to be acting in the interests of their country, to merely 'know in their hearts' that they are right. As the deliberative democrats Amy Gutmann and Dennis Thompson point out, these leaders may in fact be wrong, and without the public justification and public scrutiny of their decisions others cannot effectively judge whether they are right or wrong. As a result, these same leaders may be regarded as less trustworthy, further entrenching political disengagement.[37]

Public justification, deliberation and debate cannot in themselves make bad outcomes good, or corrupt leaders honest. The suggestion is more simply that deliberation and debate are better than their alternatives.[38] A well-informed and engaged citizenry is more likely to join in public debate and deliberation in order to ensure that their government arrives at just and good decisions. This sort of deliberation and the demand for public justification of political decisions provides an important check against the sort of limited, majoritarian democracy that sees law and policy formed on the basis of the preferences of the majority, with few protections for minority voices.[39] As Gutmann and Thompson argue: 'Those who are certain that justice is on their side should at least recognise that imposing this view on others requires a further step: trying to persuade those others that there are good reasons for this view.'[40]

Many theorists, from Rousseau to the present, have argued that participation and deliberation not only allow citizens to actually exercise some degree of influence, but also provide a form of civics education that can help to develop the capacity of all citizens to 'consider political issues in a more public-spirited mode'.[41] There are important reasons to consider alternatives to the constraining, revisionist democracy currently being practised in Australia. Participation and deliberation are crucial elements in a healthy and embracing democracy. Democracy itself derives its essential rationale from the idea that citizens give their consent to be governed.[42] A dumbed-down and disengaged population cannot give this consent, allowing the creeping authoritarianism evident in the Coalition Government to continue to develop unchecked.

Conclusion

In mid-2006 Prime Minister Howard claimed in parliament that his is the most accountable executive since Federation. Critics counter this claim with the view that, although the successive Howard governments have become the most powerful since Federation, due particularly to the centralisation of power around the office of the Prime Minister himself, there is little evidence that this has been accompanied by an increase in checks and balances or public justification and scrutiny of government activity.[43] There is abundant evidence of this decline in account-ability in the following chapters; enough, it is hoped, to cause concern among all Australian citizens, regardless of ideology or party affiliation.

Democracy may not be the robust system of government we all assume it to be. There is evidence that it must be 'handled carefully' because, in Maddox's words, the 'frail filaments of democracy are easily severed, especially by the undermining of mutual trust, the disregard of the truth and the lack of respect for those who may disagree with one's point of view'.[44] The con-tinuing effort required to preserve democratic institutions cannot be underestimated.

Howard himself would probably dismiss the theorising in this chapter. He has done much in his term in office to construct and then denigrate an imagined category of 'elites' who are out of touch with the wants and needs of aspirational 'mainstream' Aus-tralia. Arguments about the nature and quality of Australian democracy, he would perhaps contend, are beyond the everyday concerns of middle Australia.

At least, that is how he would like middle Australia to think. The authors in this book suggest differently. The concerns raised in the following chapters are very much the concern of the average Australian. Every Australian citizen deserves a democracy in which our universities and broader research community are at the cutting edge of new ideas and free of ideological intervention; we deserve a public service and statutory authorities that are free to provide frank and fearless advice without worrying about retribution; we deserve a media that is committed to, and enabled in, its work of communicating political decisions to the general public without bias or interference; we deserve a non-government sector that is properly resourced and unafraid to provide a critical voice in public policy debates; we deserve military and intelligence services that are able to place national security above political loyalty at all times; and we deserve parliamentary institutions like the Senate that provide an effective check on executive power.

Anything less is anti-democratic.

3

Universities

Stuart Macintyre

Each November, as the teaching semester draws to a close in the country's universities and academics complete the assessment of students, they are also awaiting the announcement of their own results in a particularly gruelling form of peer assessment.

Earlier in the year they submitted applications for funding from the Australian Research Council (ARC). They set out their applications in detailed proposals of thirty pages or more, carefully composed to explain the project, indicate its significance, feasibility, timeliness and national benefit, and to make the most of their research record and capacity.

The ARC receives more than four thousand of these applications each year and assigns them to expert assessors. Its 'college of experts', made up of leading authorities in the relevant disciplines, then considers the assessors' reports, along with the responses of the applicants, and makes a final determination. The decisions are then sent to the Commonwealth minister for approval and release.

Much hangs on the results. Australia has a poor record in business support for university research, and those companies that do make such investment seek quick returns from a restricted range of projects that can demonstrate clear commercial benefits. The universities have limited funds of their own for supporting research and generally use them to support external grant recipients. Each year the ARC allocates about $400 million in new funding through its various grant programs, and of this sum about $200 million goes to the projects undertaken by individuals and groups across the full range of disciplines, with the remainder going to centres. The competition is fierce: only one applicant in four is successful.

The decisions of the ARC are vital to the career prospects of the applicants. They determine which researchers will be able to undertake major research projects with appropriate personnel and equipment, and they shape publication records, employment opportunities and chances of promotion. Grant outcomes feed into the Commonwealth's formulae for funding universities, the allocation of postgraduate places and scholarships, and the various rankings of research standing on which the universities' national and international reputations rest.

Mindful of these consequences, the ARC has strict rules to guide its peer assessment. The college of experts is carefully composed to balance disciplines and avoid any concentration of members from a particular university. The procedures guard against any conflict of interest. You cannot be involved in assessing—indeed you have to absent yourself from consideration of—an application from a colleague, friend, former student or collaborator. All decisions are based strictly on merit and are carefully documented.

But in 2004 and 2005 the then minister for Education, Science and Training violated the integrity of the ARC's procedures. In 2004, Brendan Nelson, who held the portfolio from 2001 to 2006, intervened to veto three grants awarded in the humanities. He did not explain his interference—he did not even acknowledge it—but he did let Andrew Bolt, the right-wing columnist for the Melbourne *Herald-Sun*, know of his actions.

In the previous year Andrew Bolt had used his column to ridicule a number of the new projects funded by the ARC as a waste of taxpayers' money and an indulgence of political correctness. His criticism was directed at the humanities and social sciences where, he claimed, the ARC had fallen into the hands of 'a club of scratch-my-back leftists' whose work was 'hostile to our culture, history and institutions', as well as 'peek-in-your-pants researchers fixated on gender or race'.[1]

Bolt's abuse apparently struck a chord with some senior members of the Cabinet who mocked Brendan Nelson for his inability to control his portfolio. Since this minister was tireless in his populism, forever insisting that he had to satisfy a Geraldton plumber of every cent spent on higher education, he was discomforted and immediately carpeted Vicky Sara, the chief executive of the ARC.[2] His veto of the 2004 grants was thus designed to avert any repetition of Bolt's criticism or his own private embarrassment—and the briefing of Bolt played to the vanity of the columnist, who duly congratulated himself on his influence.[3]

While Nelson was only too anxious to let Andrew Bolt know of his interference, he put nothing on the public record. The staff of the ARC knew of the minister's actions but they were bound by public service rules and were still trying, behind the scenes, to minimise the damage. Those he victimised were not informed but there were rumours late in 2004 that up to five projects had been rejected. When journalists covering higher education took up the story the chair of the ARC's board said he didn't know why there was such 'hue and cry' since the statute gave the minister the power to 'intervene' if he didn't believe that taxpayers' money should be spent on 'that kind of research'. 'It doesn't happen a lot', he added, and when it did, 'one shouldn't get one's knickers in a knot'.[4]

The chair of the ARC Board was Tim Besley, a senior public servant who had gone into the private sector, chaired the board of the Commonwealth Bank and other leading companies, and served as chancellor of Macquarie University and president of the Australian Academy of Technological Sciences and Engineering. In 2006 Besley would come to greater prominence as the chair of another statutory agency, the Wheat Export Authority, which so conspicuously failed to monitor the actions of the Australian Wheat Board.

His pliancy disturbed those within the research community who knew something of the background and appreciated the gravity of such interference. It was no comfort to learn that Amanda Vanstone had rejected funding of an Indigenous research project during her brief and undistinguished responsibility for the portfolio in the 1990s. Nor did her blithe response to a subsequent request for clarification, 'Yes, I think I did', allay concern.[5]

A pro-vice chancellor for research and former senior officer of the ARC regretted the intrusion of politics into grant allocations. The president of the Council of Humanities, Arts and Social Sciences echoed his concerns and Gavin Brown, the vice-chancellor of the University of Sydney, suggested the minister's actions had worrying implications for academic freedom.[6] The

Labor opposition followed the issue but was deterred from raising it by the intimation that Brendan Nelson would use parliamentary privilege to deride the projects he had vetoed.

His successful bluff encouraged the minister to go further. Early in 2005 he requested the ARC to establish a 'Community Standards Committee' to vet the decisions of its expert panels. Rebuffed by the ARC's board, he then appointed three lay members to one of its committees, which is meant to ensure consistency of judgement across the panels, and changed its terms of reference to include consideration of national benefit. The three new members were the former High Court judge Sir Daryl Dawson, the editor of *Quadrant*, P.P. McGuinness, and the television newsreader Ross Symonds. For good measure Nelson announced in July 2005 that the board of the ARC would be abolished so he could henceforth exercise direct ministerial control.[7]

Who suggested P.P. McGuinness as one of the new appointments to the ARC's Quality and Scrutiny Committee? Probably not Brendan Nelson, since he has little to do with the obsessive ideologues who cluster around *Quadrant*. The narcissistic former minister for Education is not an ideologue but an opportunist who will say or do whatever brings praise.

McGuinness was also badly briefed. He accepted his appointment in the expectation that he would be able to inspect and reject individual applications. On learning that the committee would consider no more than the titles and summaries of the applications recommended for funding, he threatened to resign. 'Quite frankly,' he complained to a reporter in September 2005, 'it's purely window dressing.' He could tell from the titles that many of these projects were 'rubbish'.[8] The minister again intervened and directed the ARC to give McGuinness the full text of any application he wished to pursue.[9]

After exercising this prerogative, McGuinness wanted to veto many of the grants that had been determined by the college of experts. By now he was at loggerheads with other members of the committee, and Peter Hoj, the new chief executive of the ARC, warned him that 'it would be very difficult to give effect to your views if they are not adequately documented and supported by detailed comments'.[10] Accordingly, McGuinness wrote a report on the projects he wanted to axe on the understanding it would be given to the minister.

McGuinness wanted to overturn no fewer than 27 individual project grants, and the ARC scrambled to save these and rewrite the titles and descriptions of others in order to make them more palatable to the minister and his minions. Brendan Nelson disallowed three of the grants identified by McGuinness and a further four to which he took objection. None of the seven has ever been identified.

This time, however, there would be no cover-up. How could there be when McGuinness boasted of his influence? 'Clearly they were either silly or ill-designed projects,' he told a reporter. Asked how he was able to make such judgements, he replied that, 'I'm well qualified in economics and in related subjects'. But was he not undermining the process of peer review on which every system of national competitive grants rests? 'In a way, yes,' he responded, 'I'm not entirely happy about it as I don't think I understand what the process is about in full.'[11]

And this time the minister's actions brought widespread criticism. The Australian Vice-Chancellors' Committee and the Group of Eight leading research universities both condemned his arbitrary intervention and lack of transparency. The four learned academies all expressed concern that he had put at risk the country's research reputation, and well they might after several of the international experts who provide the ARC with expert advice talked of boycotting future requests to assess applications.[12]

Vicky Sara, the former chief executive of the ARC, broke her silence to note that Australia's research standing was based on its peer-review system and 'political interference in that process would damage our international reputation'. A researcher at La Trobe University who came to Australia from Russia in 1994 and had previously worked in the Soviet Academy of Sciences in Moscow said that the Commonwealth minister's action 'strikes a familiar chord'.[13]

Nelson continued to refuse all requests for an explanation. Pressed by the University of Melbourne's Glyn Davis, in his capacity as chair of the Group of Eight, to reveal the cancelled grants and the basis on which he had cancelled them, the minister replied simply that Section 51 of the *Australian Research Councils Act 2001* gave him authority to approve all proposals for funding.[14] By now, however, Tim Besley conceded that the minister's intervention might make it more difficult to attract expert assessors to serve the ARC; and, with elegant economy, Peter Hoj said he understood the desirability of transparency.[15] In February 2006, when Hoj told a Senate Estimates Committee that the minister had informed the ARC of the reason for his vetoing the seven grants (they were 'not of national benefit'), he was at pains to make clear that neither he nor his staff had been party to any conversations between the minister and McGuinness.[16]

Restricting academic freedom

At the end of 2005 I wrote an article for *The Age* and the *Sydney Morning Herald* that related the background to Nelson's actions and drew attention to his sensitivity to the views of Andrew Bolt.[17] The response astonished me. I received more than a hundred letters, phone calls and emails, and not just from academic colleagues and friends, but parliamentarians, journalists and others deeply concerned about the implications of this suppression of academic research.

Many of the researchers related their own experience of problems in pursuing projects on sensitive topics, but a recurring theme of the correspondence was particularly disturbing. They talked of my 'courage' in speaking out, related their own dismay and uncertainty about how to respond, and expressed gratitude for my 'brave article'. 'I don't suppose it will make your life any easier', one suggested. At this time it was not clear just how many grants had fallen victim to the minister; estimates ranged between four and nineteen.[18] At least a score of my correspondents were convinced they were among the victims.

As one of the more persistent higher education reporters noted at the time, Brendan Nelson's silence augmented the effect of his actions.[19] If a regimen of censorship suppresses dissent, an arbitrary and secretive exercise of the censor's powers inhibits the willingness to risk dissidence—so that a number of my correspondents indicated that they would no longer submit applications on contentious topics. The surrender of academic freedom is far more insidious than the attack on it.

The present government's interference in the ARC is only one of the ways in which it has politicised the public funding of research. On coming to office in 1996 the Howard Government closed the Bureau of Immigration and Population Research, which it evidently regarded as a hotbed of multiculturalism. At the same time it cancelled a contract with the Centre for Immigration and Multicultural Studies at the Australian National University, which supported the preparation of a new edition of James Jupp's authoritative *Encyclopedia of the Australian People*.[20]

It subjected other university centres conducting research in areas of public policy to unprecedented surveillance. There are a number of centres supported by various Commonwealth departments on the understanding that their research is of public benefit. The academic freedom of these centres is clearly vital to the work they undertake. The government has a legitimate interest in ensuring that they operate efficiently, that the projects they pursue are relevant and that their findings are robust, but if such research is to have value then it needs to be conducted without interference. The appropriate arrangement is a funding agreement that specifies the functions of the centre, its structure and operating details, and typically provides for an external review of performance; beyond that the centre should be free to conduct and publish its research.

One necessary safeguard is that appointments to such centres are made according to the usual selection procedures for an academic position: by open advertisement and judgement on merit against appropriate selection criteria. In 1998 the Commonwealth provided annual funding of $1 million for the establishment of a Centre for Democratic Institutions at the Australian National University. A selection committee chose Dr John Uhr, a highly qualified political scientist, as the director of the centre. That decision was then put to Minister for Foreign Affairs Alexander

Downer for approval, and it is alleged that he then consulted the Prime Minister. In the event a former Australian ambassador, Mr Roland Rich, who had no research qualifications, was appointed the foundation director.[21]

A further danger of such arrangements is that they enable the government to bypass the normal processes for evaluating the merits of a proposal. The 2006 federal Budget included an appropriation of $22 million for an Adult Stem Cell Centre at Griffith University. The research director of the institute where the centre will be located had been invited to seek this funding by Minister for Health Tony Abbott. The minister was on record for his religious concerns over embryonic stem cell research, and direct funding of an alternative centre to work on adult stem cells allowed him to avoid the rigorous peer assessment of the merits of the proposal had it been considered by the National Health and Medical Research Council (NHMRC).[22]

Still other such research centres have been created as the result of political deals. In 1999 the government relied on the support of Meg Lees, the leader of the Australian Democrats, to secure the passage of the goods and services tax legislation through the Senate. Part of the price was the establishment of a Centre for Child Welfare at the University of South Australia, in the state she represented. Regardless of the merits of the centre, its location was decided on purely political grounds.[23]

Particularly disturbing cases of interference have occurred when the minister or ministerial advisers have objected to the work undertaken in research centres. In 1980 the Fraser Government helped establish the Social Policy Research Centre (SPRC) at the University of New South Wales. It built up a strong reputation over the following two decades, and the government funding was continued after three external reviews in 1984, 1988–89 and 1993–94. As part of its activity, the SPRC began a study in 1995 into the adequacy of income support levels that was designed to inform changes in social security benefits. The Howard Government was unhappy about this project, especially when it revealed that income needs were higher than benefit levels, and the SPRC's director, Professor Peter Saunders, was called to Canberra and warned of the need for careful management of the findings.

The SPRC was due for a further review in 1998, but Jocelyn Newman, then minister for Social Security, would not accept the reviewers the university proposed. When the review team was finally assembled it gave strong endorsement to the work of the centre—as indeed did officers of the Department of Social Security—and recommended the Commonwealth funding should be maintained. The minister rejected that recommendation, opting instead for a competitive tender. The amount the SPRC won was little more than a third of the earlier grant, and its new contract required prior government approval for every project the centre undertook with the reduced funding. Saunders found the treatment 'totally devastating' and is 'still recovering from the sense of despair over the simple unfairness of the whole process'.[24]

Another centre, the Centre for Aboriginal Economic Policy Research (CAEPR) at the Australian National University, incurred even greater displeasure when it challenged the outcomes of the government's policy of 'practical reconciliation'. Even though its study, which was published in a reputable economics journal in 2003, used census data to support the conclusions, the Commonwealth agency that funded CAEPR posted a hostile response to the study on its website. A year later the centre was instructed to remove a report on another project from its own website, and to postpone a seminar on the project. Finally, in 2005 when CAEPR was commissioned by Oxfam to assess the likely effects of the Commonwealth's proposed changes to land rights, the Commonwealth agency instructed the Australian Federal Police to investigate the university for allegedly divulging a confidential government document and with a clear implication that the researchers who received a particular document may face criminal charges. Two months later the government informed the CAEPR that its core funding would end.[25]

What responsibility should universities accept for these alarming abuses of academic independence? Without knowing precisely what happened in the negotiations with the government in the particular cases, it is nevertheless clear that the university officers could have done more to protect the integrity of their procedures. And since similar government expectations would seem to have applied to many other such special-purpose funding arrangements characterised by a cosy compliancy, it is tempting to conclude that universities should maintain an arm's length relationship in their dealings with government.

But this is to ignore the circumstances in which universities are now forced to operate. They used to be small, privileged, civic institutions teaching a professional elite and conducting a restricted range of specialised research. They are now large, complex, closely managed enterprises essential to vocational training and the information economy. For a quarter of a century public funding has lagged behind the expansion of activity, so that universities have become dependent on fees and other sources of income. The block grants that used to support their research have been diverted to the ARC and NHMRC. These funding agencies are expected in turn to serve national objectives. The government specifies research priorities, ties many of the grants to industry partnerships and expects universities to commercialise their intellectual property.

Meanwhile these universities are competing with each other, and with overseas institutions, for students, staff and research support. It is small wonder that they welcome partnerships with government departments and the private sector, or that their established collegial procedures to safeguard academic integrity should come under strain. The growing regimen of quality assurance, ethics committees and reporting requirements testifies to the problem—and rather than safeguard academic freedom, these new forms of invigilation often displace it.

The decline since the Menzies era

As the Commonwealth's contribution to university expenditure has fallen, so its regulation of the universities has increased. The Department of Education, Science and Training now demands an extraordinary volume of data to enforce compliance with its requirements. In the 1940s, when the Commonwealth first began funding universities, an astute statesman appreciated that there was a grave risk that in accepting this support the universities would lose their independence.

Robert Menzies was a reluctant supporter of Commonwealth funding, partly because he was a traditionalist who believed universities should remain sheltered places of higher learning, partly because he was a federalist reluctant to trespass on a state function, but most of all because he wanted to safeguard a 'proper freedom of teaching and research'.[26] A decade later, when he came to see the need for more adequate provision, Menzies took care to appoint a committee of inquiry that shared his concern.

The report of the Murray Committee affirmed precisely this understanding of academic freedom. It began with the explanation that universities 'possessed a high degree of autonomy and self-determination on the ground that the particular services which they render, both to their own country and to mankind in general, cannot be rendered without such freedom'. There was a pressing need for more graduates, but 'the function of the university [was] to offer not merely a technical or specialist training but a full and true education, befitting a free man and the citizen of a free country'.[27]

The committee registered the growing importance of research but insisted that the greatest advances in knowledge came 'because free inquirers have been pursuing their own ideas and insights, devotedly and with great persistence, in pursuit of enlightenment for its own sake'. Finally, the Murray Committee declared that the university must provide the 'guardians of intellectual standards and intellectual integrity in the community' to 'be proof against the waves of emotion and prejudice which make the ordinary man, and public opinion, subject from time to time to illusion and self-conceit'.[28]

The government needed the university just as the university needed the support of government, and it was appropriate that universities should consider the national interest, but the committee was confident that 'no Australian Government will seek to deny them their full and free independence in carrying out their proper functions as universities'.[29] The Menzies Government therefore established the Australian Universities Commission as an independent body that would allocate triennial grants for teaching and research.

But in the year of Menzies' retirement, this happy arrangement began to break down. In 1966 the government rejected the commission's recommended grants for the next triennium, and thereafter the commission became increasingly prescriptive. By 1987, when John Dawkins took over the education portfolio, he imposed a series of mergers, management changes, personnel procedures and educational requirements on what was now a Uniform National System.

Lying behind these intrusions on university autonomy was government disappointment over the failure to increase participation rates in higher education and an equal disappointment with the failure to generate economic growth through teaching and research. It became common to criticise the universities for their self-serving complacency, and the stock response was to impose a closer control over their operations. The Australian Universities Commission has long since disappeared, and the department now directly administers universities across the whole range of their activities.

But Menzies could scarcely have foreseen the lengths to which the present government would go with its proscription of student unions or its refusal to allow universities to determine their own industrial relations. That Liberal leader had insisted that the Commonwealth's grants should be free of conditions in order to safeguard the proper freedom of teaching and research; his successors use the funding mechanism to impose their own prejudices.

Conclusion

Brendan Nelson left the Ministry of Education, Science and Training in March 2006 and Julie Bishop, his successor, has signalled that she intends to be less interventionist: 'My view is that if the peer review system has the independence and integrity to ensure that it's robust, then I would see no need for me to second-guess that process'.[30] But the government has persisted with its legislation to abolish the ARC Board and give the minister direct control over its activities. The *Australian Research Council Amendment Act 2006* allows the minister to establish any committee or dissolve it at any time, to terminate the appointment of any member at any time, and to direct its operations.

The criticism of publicly funded research is not new. Back in the 1980s the Liberal opposition formed a Waste Watch Committee to comb through the annual announcement of grants made by the Australian Research Grants Committee (the predecessor of the ARC), and deride projects in the humanities and social sciences for their esoteric character. But Barry Jones and later John Dawkins, the ministers responsible for university research at that time, defended the independence of the ARGC and insisted on the need for funding research on the basis of peer assessment.

Nor was the criticism peculiar to Australia. In 1975 the United States Senator William Proxmire invented the Golden Fleece Award for wasteful public expenditure and conferred the first award on the country's principal research agency, the National Science Foundation, because it had provided a grant of $84 000 for a study of why people fall in love. But these Golden Fleece Awards were bestowed liberally across a wide range of items in the federal Budget, from the postal service's advertising campaigns to the executive fleet of the Air Force.[31] And while the Reagan Administration reduced the NSF's budget for research in the social sciences, it did not interfere with the integrity of the grant-determination process.

The Thatcher Government waged a similar campaign against the British agency, the Social Sciences Research Council, for funding left-wing researchers and supporting arcane projects—the example singled out for ridicule there was a study of village life in Poland. But Lord Rothschild, whom the government appointed to conduct an inquiry, warned that 'to dismember or liquidate the Council would be an act of intellectual vandalism with damaging consequences for the whole country'.[32] In the event the budget was cut and its name was changed (it became the Economic and Social Research Council) to eliminate the reference to science, but the government stopped short of direct interference.

Unlike Australia, the United States, the United Kingdom and indeed all countries with reputable research arrangements see the need for a buffer between the paymasters and investigators. If a national competitive grant system is to have any meaning, the competition must be on the basis of intellectual merit and not political palatability. Brendan Nelson's wanton disregard for the necessary safeguards placed Australia's research reputation at risk. His overturning of the ARC's decisions was compounded by the denial of any form of accountability for his actions, and has now been put on a permanent institutional basis by the removal of its autonomy.

Academic freedom is not a natural state of affairs. It took long struggles to liberate universities from coercion, and the various meanings that are embodied in the concept of academic freedom have never been straightforward, always subject to changing expectations and pressures. Even so, the recent assault on academic freedom in Australia has been marked.

One reason is that present appeals to academic freedom are not necessarily persuasive. Academic freedom rests on the idea of self-regulation, allowing academics to decide among themselves the work it is important for them to undertake. The protections that guarantee this freedom cover the rite of passage (senior academics control the award of the doctoral degree and then the process of recruitment to a university post), and every subsequent stage of an academic career (promotion, publication, the approval of new courses, the award of grants, election to an academy). This is a paradigm of professionalism that protects freedom of inquiry for the specialist. It is a system based on merit, but it excludes the non-academics and lays itself open to accusations of privilege, favouritism and intolerance. This is a vulnerability that Andrew Bolt exploits with his reference to 'scratch-my-back leftists' who are part of the pampered elites.

A second reason is that researchers in the humanities and social sciences have largely abandoned the claim to be engaged in a scientific search for truth. Many in the humanities understand their disciplines as involving a process of inquiry that is necessarily interpretive, neither testing a hypothesis nor producing a verifiable result, but rather offering interpretations that are always partial, perspectival and contingent. Many in the social sciences would reject the notion of intellectual inquiry as a neutral and disinterested activity. These positions do not negate the need for honesty and rigour, nor do they lessen the adherence to the professional paradigm, but they might well have weakened the epistemological foundations of academic freedom.[33]

Finally, there is a loss of academic authority. As universities have become more worldly, more integrated into the information economy, more central to skills formation and more important as an export industry, they have faced competition from alternative providers for whom the expectation of academic freedom is an obsolete irrelevance. Research institutes and private think tanks provide policy advice and advocacy with little regard to independence or objectivity. Newspaper columnists serve as a new kind of public intellectual, replacing informed commentary with vilification and abuse.

The fact that Andrew Bolt initiated the attack on the ARC and P.P. McGuinness was allowed to subvert it speaks eloquently of the degradation of this national institution. Most of all, it was betrayed by a minister who saw advantage in exploiting such prejudice and a government that seeks unprecedented control. Academic freedom, as Menzies appreciated, is not simply a privilege afforded to academics; it is the very basis of a genuine civil society and a healthy democracy.

4

The research community

Ian Lowe

The 1999 World Conference on Science in Budapest was the first UN conference on science and its applications for twenty years. Jointly organised by UNESCO and the umbrella body for national academies and learned societies, ICSU, it called for a new social contract between science and society, with a formal code of ethics for scientists along similar lines to the Hippocratic oath taken by medical graduates.[1] Nobel Laureate Joseph Rotblat called for a code of ethics; he wanted to go much further than obvious basic principles like honesty and respect for human dignity. He argued that scientists should respect the global environment and take into account our responsibility for future generations. A paper by ICSU endorsed the idea of international guidelines.[2]

The Howard Government is increasingly using science, as the old joke goes, as a drunk uses a lamppost—for support rather than for illumination. Within its main science organisation, CSIRO, there is now a culture of managerialism so wary of offending government that scientists have been instructed not to comment on issues that have policy implications. Even within universities, once prized for their principles of academic freedom and their willingness to protect academics against victimisation, there is now increasing pressure to conform. The policy line is set, often on the basis of ideology or whim rather than detailed analysis. Science is urged to get on board the policy train. Those who support it cheerfully speak out, but those who know it to be wrong are intimidated into silence. Those who know do not speak, while those who speak do not know—or, even worse, pretend not to know.

This chapter discusses some case studies of experts who have been silenced by the system. It shows how the public debate has been impoverished as a result, leading to policy directions that are not in the national interest.

Intimidating the experts

A striking example of intimidation was widely publicised in the ABC's *Four Corners* in February 2006.[3] Professor Graeme Pearman is one of Australia's most distinguished atmospheric scientists. He has been involved in the measurement of greenhouse gas concentrations and the modelling of climate change for nearly 30 years, and as a result has an outstanding international reputation in the field. Within Australia he has been recognised by election as a Fellow of both the Academy of Science and the Academy of Technological Sciences and Engineering. The CSIRO Division then headed by Pearman organised two landmark conferences in the 1980s: 'Greenhouse '87', a major scientific conference to explore the implications of the scale and rate of climate change being predicted by CSIRO models, and 'Greenhouse '88', a national conference aimed at a broader audience to increase public awareness of the problem. He has continued to communicate the science to politicians and the public alike, including briefings for many government agencies.

In 2004, Pearman was involved in a scientific initiative to draw together the disturbing evidence that climate change is already having serious impacts on Australia, with much worse in prospect if we continue to neglect the issue. The report of the Australian Climate Group, *Climate Change Solutions for Australia*, looked at environmental, economic and social impacts, including effects on community health.[4] It covered the evidence that climate change is already happening, the concerns about future developments and some suggested responses. In retrospect, these were hardly radical suggestions. By 2005 the Australian Medical Association was joining the Australian Conservation Foundation to make similar suggestions, based on analysis of the alarming consequences for public health of the current Howard Government business-as-usual strategy.[5] By early 2006 the CEOs of six large companies, including BP, Westpac and Origin Energy, were prepared to call publicly for the same sorts of measures: a long-term aspirational target of reducing greenhouse gas emissions by 60 per cent by 2050, a short-term binding target and market mechanisms to provide incentives for businesses to invest in the new technologies needed.[6]

As the group prepared for the release of the report in mid-2004 a media strategy was developed to maximise its impact, with a central role for Pearman as a leading authority. At that point he was pressured by those above him in the CSIRO hierarchy to confine his public remarks to the climate science and refrain from commenting on the policy issues. This approach was defended by Pearman's immediate CSIRO line manager, Dr Steve Morton, on *Four Corners* when he said the organisation's policy is that scientists can comment on science but not on policy.[7] This approach was seen in action when another CSIRO scientist, Dr Kevin Hennessy, was asked questions about climate change. He said that global warming is a serious problem, that it could have disastrous effects and that we know what is causing the problem, but was then placed by the CSIRO policy in the ridiculous situation of being unable to comment on which responses would be the most effective.

The message to Pearman from the CSIRO management was very clear: do your science, publish in learned journals, answer questions from the media about the technical issues of climate modelling, but do not say anything that could be interpreted by the most hyper-sensitive minister as implicitly critical of government policy. As Pearman puts it: 'As a climate scientist, I might inform [media] that the lifetime of carbon dioxide in the atmosphere means that the only way of stabilising global climate is by reducing emissions by 50 per cent by 2050 and by 80 per cent by 2100. In the current environment, that is seen as commenting on the government policy of not setting reduction targets.'[8]

CSIRO management were apparently unhappy with Pearman's public statements as part of the launch of the climate group's report, even though the report makes no specific reference to the Commonwealth government and Pearman stuck scrupulously to the limited role specified. He was subsequently made redundant, along with some other senior climate scientists in the division he had led. In fact, ten leading scientists besides Pearman have left the division in the last few years. Pearman says it was made very clear that management did not want him around, even banning him from entering the building in which he had worked for decades.

We now know that this is part of a broader pattern of the federal government making extensive efforts to control public information about the effects of climate change. The *Four Corners* program revealed that CSIRO management, under pressure from the government, has attempted to gag its scientists from speaking publicly about their research on climate change. Pearman said he was censored perhaps half a dozen times in the year before he was forced out of his position.[9]

The government seems particularly fearful of any discussion of the potential problem of environmental refugees. Another respected CSIRO scientist, Dr Barry Pittock, was instructed to remove references to environmental refugees from a report he had prepared for the government even though, conscious of political sensitivities, he had included the subject in what he called 'a very muted form'. Pittock, author of a major new book on climate change and its impacts,[10] is more vigorously involved in public discussion of the problem now that he is free of the CSIRO guidelines that muzzle government scientists.

University scientists engaged in research into renewable energy are also intimidated. According to Philip Jennings, professor of energy studies at Murdoch University, renewable energy researchers believe they will lose their research funding if they are seen to criticise federal government policies on climate change and energy.

The federal government is attempting to control the debate over greenhouse science by gagging some scientists and intimidating others. I will return to this general issue after considering the second example.

Muddling the models

Dr Barney Foran has an international reputation in the area of modelling future paths of development and their resource demands. He also found CSIRO management unwilling to defend science against government ideology.[11] The story began in the early 1990s when the CSIRO Division of Wildlife and Ecology made a strategic decision to try to introduce some science into the human population debate for Australia. The scientists' rationale was that they were studying environmental issues and problems without examining the causal issues or driving forces: for instance, spreading suburbs threatens koala habitats, increasing wheat production clears land and causes habitat loss. The Department of Immigration and Multicultural Affairs (DIMA) engaged the CSIRO group to explore the environmental, resource and infrastructure issues arising from three different projected population futures. Two DIMA officials managed the project for the federal government, while Foran led the team from CSIRO. Two risk management strategies were proposed by DIMA and accepted by the CSIRO team. The then minister, Philip Ruddock, appointed a five-person ministerial steering committee for policy oversight and due diligence. Since physical-economy analysis was new to Australia, the model assumptions and operation were examined in a series of sixteen linked workshops on topics such as population, transport, housing, water and energy, which received input from over 500 national experts in these areas. The project proceeded reasonably smoothly through the workshop and initial report drafting phases. However, once the team began to draft a synthesis, saying in plain English what the numbers really meant, project relations began to sour.

DIMA's Abul Rizvi fired off a letter to Foran's divisional chief, Dr Steve Morton. The letter attacked the credibility of the analysis on a number of issues, including the population numbers derived from the immigration inputs, as well as issues concerning unemployment, water, greenhouse emissions, oil depletion and trade balances. The subtext was the extreme unease displayed by the DIMA project officer, Neil Mullenger, when faced by these weighty national issues. A technological optimist, Mullenger kept offering Foran technical 'solutions' to the embarrassing policy dilemmas that emerged from CSIRO's model of Australia's potential futures.

In project meetings, Ruddock's steering committee had asked that the final synthesis chapter 'tell it like it really is'. However, when the conclusions showed that business-as-usual was leading to serious problems, the committee reversed its position. The impasse between immigration policy and science was resolved with an agreement between Foran's superiors, Steve Morton and Allen Kearns, and DIMA's Rizvi and Mullenger. CSIRO would delete the final synthesis chapter from the report, it would delete the unemployment analysis, it would prepare a distilled version for policy-makers, and Ruddock's steering committee would add their oversight and due diligence chapter at the end. But that wasn't the end of the story.

When this additional activity was completed to the satisfaction of both parties, DIMA rang Foran's superiors to say that they would not release the report at all. This was at odds with the project brief and discussions, which at all times had designed the project to provide an open and transparent examination of Australia's population options, 'fishhooks and all'. Foran's managers were in an awkward position, given that CSIRO seems to adopt the position that 'the client is always right'. Suppressing the report was difficult because Foran was already presenting the project outcomes as conference papers, breakfast talks and community briefings. Many draft copies of the document were out for review and information purposes. A scientific paper had been refereed and was about to appear in the Monash University journal, *People and Place*. Thus the key elements of the project were already 'out there'. News of the report's suppression reached the ABC's *Four Corners* staff, who decided to prepare a feature on it.

When reporter Ticky Fullerton began interviewing for the program, a storm of angry phone calls erupted in the Canberra bureaucracy. Realising that the cat was already out of the bag, DIMA agreed to work with CSIRO toward a joint launch in October 2002. But the department leaked the report on the Saturday before the agreed official launch date, in order to put its own spin on it. Presumably as a result of this, the *Sydney Morning Herald* led with the headline, 'We'll Be Right with 50 Million', a message that deliberately misrepresented the report's conclusions. Although the remainder of the coverage was fair, according to Foran, and extended over many pages, the misleading headline muddied the water for those who read the whole report and misled the many who did not read the entire text. The same material was reproduced in Melbourne's *Age*. CSIRO was on the back foot; Foran recalls that the weekend was spent in damage control, doing media briefings on the run.

DIMA's supporters in *The Australian* then set about destroying the credibility of the report. Prominent writers Alan Wood,

George Megalogenis and Paul Kelly had in the past made clear their support for high immigration levels. Each attacked the CSIRO report. Alan Wood's Tuesday piece, 'Narrow views on broadening population', used misinformation that was not drawn from the report but came from project steering committee meetings.[12] So specific was the information that it could only have come from DIMA officials or ministerial staffers. One DIMA official approached Foran afterwards to say that he was deeply unhappy with the comments and wanted to distance himself from the actions of his superiors.

The following Saturday, Paul Kelly's 'Deep green dilemma'[13] and George Megalogenis's 'Unleashing the dogma of science'[14] continued what looked like an orchestrated assault on the report. Unlike Wood, at least these two interviewed Foran. Paul Kelly has a consistent view on the issue of population growth. Some years later, at a conference on the issue in Canberra, he asserted that population growth is good for the economy. He was challenged in the discussion period by Dr John Coulter, the former Democrats Senator for South Australia. Coulter presented OECD figures showing that countries with rapid population growth have poorer economic performance than those that have stabilised their populations. Kelly replied, 'I haven't seen the OECD literature, but I think a lot of people would dispute what you said!' Kelly is a skilled advocate for his views, regardless of the statistical evidence to counter them. His piece was described by Foran as 'particularly nifty' in the way it took elements of the interview and juxtaposed them with other comments out of context to misrepresent the findings and Foran's views.

Those who read *The Australian* would have gained the impression that Foran's research findings were not solidly grounded in economic and social reality. In an attempt to set the record straight on the technical issues Foran wrote a 'reply to the critics' article for the journal *People and Place*. This was peer reviewed and approved for publication by his line management at CSIRO. It was undergoing final typesetting at the journal when an obviously uncomfortable Dr Steve Morton led a delegation of five people from the CSIRO Corporate Centre to Foran's office to express management concern about the publication. Why did this tame technical response alarm CSIRO's managers? The organisation was at the time negotiating its three-year funding agreement with the Howard Government and seemed wary of offending it. Managers were particularly concerned at the risk of annoying someone as influential as Paul Kelly at *The Australian*. Foran was told to withdraw the manuscript. The managing editor of *People and Place*, Dr Bob Birrell, was incensed at the disruption to his publishing timetable. He was equally concerned about this control of the right to publish, central to inquiry and scholarship. Birrell wrote to the chair of the CSIRO Board, asking whether CSIRO would like to see this issue portrayed on the front page of every national daily. The organisation relented and an amended article was published.

Foran now reflects on the whole experience. He believes the government 'thought police' are, if anything, even more active and effective, as shown by the *Four Corners* documentary on the global climate change debate, discussed earlier. Those responsible for censoring and discrediting the report have prospered professionally. DIMA's Abul Rizvi is now a deputy secretary at the department, and has been rewarded with a Public Service Medal and a Centenary of Federation Medal for his services to immigration. Dr Steve Morton, the uncomfortable leader of the management team, is a deputy CEO at CSIRO and responsible for a wide range of decisions on research strategy.

Funding science and innovation

Since the election of the Howard Government in 1996, spending on research and innovation has declined.[15] One public policy initiative of previous ALP governments had succeeded in boosting private sector investment in research: a 150 per cent tax concession. The first Howard-Costello Budget reduced the concession to 125 per cent, effectively doubling the real cost to private companies of doing research and development. As would have been expected, the increasing cost reduced demand, and private sector research spending fell and has never recovered. Public funding of science has continued to decline as a fraction of both GDP and government outlays, at a time when most OECD countries are investing in new knowledge as the basis of economic advancement. Australia now ranks among the bottom few countries of the OECD, alongside Turkey, Iceland, Greece and Portugal, in the level of investment in science. The effect of the decline in funding has been to intensify the competition for limited funds. This increases the pressure to refrain from any criticism that might antagonise those controlling the purse strings.

The Cooperative Research Centres (CRC) program was established by Professor Ralph Slatyer when he was the government chief scientist. It was an imaginative initiative to address a long-standing problem in Australia: the repeated failure to turn our excellent science into practical innovations. Slatyer argued that all the incentives in universities and government laboratories encouraged pure science, leading to publishing in scholarly journals. Working with partners to turn research results into practical applications, either commercial ventures or developments in the public interest, is difficult and often unrewarded. His proposal was based on the adage that trying to direct academic researchers is like trying to herd cats—but you can make cats go where you want with a bowl of cream. The CRC scheme provided attractive research funding for proposals that brought together scientists with organisations that could turn the research results into practical applications—corporations, industry groups or public agencies. In the early rounds, there was a healthy balance between commercial projects and those aimed at the public interest. It funded, for example, a Centre for Renewable Energy. Other significant public-interest centres worked on integrated pest management, tropical rainforests, the Great Barrier Reef and the coastal zone. One by one, every one of those centres saw its funding end. The CRC program has moved increasingly toward commercial outcomes.

These changes are significant because the perception of what constitutes the public interest is intensely political. So funding research in the public interest leads inevitably to debate about where that interest lies. By steering research funds away from activities promoting the public interest, the government has replaced the concept of the public interest with an economistic view, implicitly equating the good of the private sector with the good of the community. Of course, the change also steers research funds away from those dedicated individuals who were working for the public good rather than commercial gain, muzzling them from participating in public debate.

Stacking the deck

The Coalition Government made it clear very early that it intended to make appointments to advisory bodies on an overtly political basis. I experienced this at first hand. Having been appointed to various advisory bodies by ministers in the Hawke and Keating governments, I found myself systematically disappointed from one body after another. Some of the changes were quite explicitly political, rather than the result of considered reflection and weighing of alternatives. For example, the government was so determined to remove Dr Peter Pockley and me from the advisory council of the National Science and Technology Centre (Questacon) that it went ahead without having found replacements, leaving the council short-handed for several months. More recently, I expressed interest in an advisory body that was clearly in my field of expertise. The government had established an exemplary process for considering expressions of interest, with an advisory group representing obvious interests and chaired by an independent academic. I left the interview feeling positive about my application. When I was not appointed, several members of the advisory group told me independently that I had been ranked very highly, but their advice had been rejected at the political level.

Whole advisory bodies were axed. The previous government had established the National Greenhouse Advisory Panel. Chaired by a distinguished academic engineer, Professor Paul Greenfield, it brought together a diverse group of experts representing the coal, oil, electricity and gas industries, unions, consumers, government and the scientific community. In 1997, this group was asked to advise the government on its review of the National

Greenhouse Response Strategy, developed five years earlier by the then ALP Government. Stripped of the more tactful wording, the panel essentially said that the sentiments and proposed strategies in the response strategy were fine and just needed to be implemented. The silence from Canberra was deafening. The NGAP was never again asked to meet. We were never formally disbanded, never even insincerely thanked by the responsible minister for our work and invited to cease our work; we just never met again. From time to time I would bump into the chair in an airport or at a university function and find him as bemused as I was by the extraordinary situation. Some years later, he was told informally that the government believed its establishment of the National Greenhouse Office within the Canberra bureaucracy removed the need for external advice on the subject.[16] It would take an extremely charitable observer to conclude that the government has such an exemplary strategic approach to the problem of global climate change that it would not benefit from engagement of a broader range of interests and opinions. The government was given good but unwelcome advice, and responded by getting rid of the advisory body.

The honouring of those who have made significant environmental contributions is another area where the government has moved to control the process, thus sending a clear message that criticism will not be tolerated. In the year 2000, Australia hosted the United Nations Environmental Program awards at a glittering lunch in Adelaide. The government marked the occasion by establishing a series of Prime Minister's awards. I was informed by those managing the process that I had been nominated for the award for outstanding individual achievement and was invited to submit a curriculum vitae for the independent panel to consider.

Ray Moynihan, writing in *Good Weekend Magazine* in 2005, reported that the panel decided I should be named the Prime Minister's Environmentalist of the Year, but were then told by the Prime Minister's office to reconsider and choose somebody else.[17] According to Moynihan, the panel stuck to their guns, so I received the award.

However, the incident so incensed the government that it changed the process for following years, removing the independent panel and controlling the choice itself. This account in no way reflects on the people who have been honoured in subsequent years, but rather on the government's unhealthy desire to control the process. Of course, the story of the first award eventually leaked into the media, making it clear that I would not have been honoured if the current process had been in operation. This sent a clear message to any who might be in the running for the award: being critical of the Howard Government or its environmental policies will rule them out. In 2006 the Prime Minister's Environmentalist of the Year award went not to a person but an organisation, the Australian Wildlife Conservancy, a private body devoted to creating fenced wildlife sanctuaries. It is a worthy but politically very safe organisation. Its CEO is Atticus Fleming, who was formerly on the staff of Senator Robert Hill when he was Environment minister in the Howard Government.

The nuclear task force

In 2006, the Prime Minister went on an extravagant overseas tour widely, although incorrectly, interpreted as a 'lap of honour' before a possible retirement. Having apparently been encouraged by Washington to stitch Australia more firmly into the nuclear industry, he returned and announced the establishment of a task force to advise the government on this issue. The group was clearly put together on the run, because the Prime Minister faced the media unable to give the full membership; three names were announced then and a further three the following day. The group is heavily oriented toward the nuclear industry, being chaired by Dr Ziggy Switkowski, who was at the time on the board of the Australian Nuclear Science and Technology Organisation (ANSTO). ANSTO is a vigorous and outspoken proponent of Australia's further involvement in the nuclear industry. It has funded research on uranium enrichment and radioactive waste management, actively urging support of those activities. The current head of ANSTO, Dr Ian Smith, addressed a public forum in Brisbane in April 2006 and urged the gathering to see nuclear power as a desirable component of our future energy supply. ANSTO had commissioned a report from a carefully chosen UK consultant to make the bizarre claim that nuclear power could be economic in Australia. The fine print noted that this would require huge public subsidies, but there was no such qualification in ANSTO's public pronouncements that nuclear was 'cost-effective' and 'greenhouse-friendly'.

Appointing a member of the ANSTO Board to chair the 'independent' inquiry into nuclear power is like appointing an office-bearer of Right to Life to conduct an independent inquiry into abortion. Following strong public criticism Dr Switkowski decided it would look better if he 'stood aside from the ANSTO Board while chairing the task force', but that is as effective a guarantee of independence as if the hypothetical Right to Life official stood aside from that organisation while conducting their 'independent' inquiry. Satirist John Clark described the task force as 'an independent group of people who think we should have nuclear power by Tuesday'. The other two members of the group announced at the media conference were professors George Dracoulis and Warwick McKibbin of the Australian National University. Dracoulis is on record as supporting use of nuclear power.[18] McKibbin is an economist, in favour in Canberra because he publicly criticised the Kyoto Agreement to curb production of greenhouse gases.[19] No member of the group had been critical of the government's approach to energy or global climate change. It was difficult to escape the conclusion that the group had been hand-picked because its members' views accord with those of the government.

Conclusion

The depressing conclusion is that the present government has gone to extraordinary lengths to silence independent opinion within the research community. Individual academics, the university system as a whole, government research organisations and individual scientists now practise what a colleague called 'the pre-emptive crumble', falling over before they are pushed and taking great care not to antagonise Canberra. Given the huge problems we face we need to encourage new ideas and support challenges to conventional wisdom, not suppress them. Most senior people I know in industry and commerce support that view. Dr Graeme Pearman quoted one as saying, in reference to the research community: 'What industry wants is independent and fearless advice.'[20] So would a government concerned about our future.

As a person who has been forced by the scientific evidence to conclude that the current approach has quite fundamental problems, I see the silencing of independent, expert opinion as a national tragedy. The government's short-sighted policies are systematically depriving our society of the innovations and new knowledge we need to avert our continuing environmental decline.

5

Non-government organisations

Sarah Maddison and Clive Hamilton

Non-government organisations (NGOs) have been an indispensable part of Australian society and politics for decades. Organisations such as the Red Cross, the Brotherhood of St Lawrence, Oxfam and the Australian Conservation Foundation, along with thousands of smaller organisations all around the country, are admired and respected not just for the services they deliver to marginalised and disadvantaged groups but for their contribution to public debate and the democratic process.

There are as many as 700 000 organisations that make up Australia's diverse not-for-profit sector, including sporting clubs, surf-lifesaving associations, churches, private schools, reading groups and so on.[1] Most of these organisations are not generally considered by governments to pose any direct threat to their authority. Many provide social services, education and research, cultural and recreational activities, health services, and employment and sectoral support through business and professional associations and unions. But included in this broad grouping is a subset of organisations that consider they have an important role—in part or in whole—as 'extra-parliamentary representative bodies' or policy advocates.[2] This chapter is concerned with the threats to this advocacy aspect of NGO work including the lobbying, consultation and advice activities that make a direct contribution to the debates that inform our public policy processes.[3]

Debate is fundamental to the development of good public policy. Good policy must reflect a range of perspectives and be based on knowledge of real people's lives and experiences. NGOs are the repository of an enormous amount of information about how things work in their part of the world and governments today simply cannot make effective policy without access to that bank of knowledge. At times this will mean that governments must endure public criticism of their policies and programs. Despite the discomfort that this process may produce, a mature government with a commitment to a robust and deliberative democracy must recognise that criticism from NGOs provides a kind of feedback loop by which they can be informed of problems or inadequacies in their development and implementation of policies and programs. Advice from those organisations closest to the problem will help governments provide the best services and develop the best policies for all members of a society.

Successive government inquiries have endorsed this view of NGOs as providing an essential contribution to Australian democracy. In 1991 the House of Representatives Standing Committee on Community Affairs (HORSCCA) reported on its inquiry into the funding of peak health and community organisations. The report recommended continued Commonwealth funding 'on the basis that public education, public debate and community consultation assist the development of appropriate policies and programs, especially where disadvantaged groups are concerned'.[4] In 1995, the Industry Commission inquired into the role of charitable organisations. The announcement of this inquiry had caused much concern in the NGO sector due to the fact that the commission was seen by many NGOs as 'an instrument of neo-classical economic surgery'.[5] Nevertheless the Industry Commision report, like the HORSCCA report, recognised the legitimate role of peak community sector organisations as 'representative organisations' that provide 'advocacy and representation (among other duties) . . . for its members and other interested parties'.[6]

In 1996 a further independent review of peak non-government organisations by RPR Organisational Consultants provided a more detailed inventory of the sector's democratic contributions, suggesting that NGOs:

- provide access to the views of disadvantaged or marginalised groups to improve the development and design of policy and programs;
- provide expertise and knowledge about the needs and circumstances of specific groups in the community;
- promote public debate needed for good policy;
- offer an efficient source of national dialogue on issues that cross state and territory boundaries;
- assist in the process of accountability of government to the wider community by providing feedback on the effects of policy; and
- present important perspectives and information which can counter or balance the views put forward by other organised interests, such as business groups.[7]

It also suggested NGOs can facilitate wider community under-standing of policies. These views are echoed in a wide range of academic and other research that notes the importance of the non-government sector in liberal democracies. NGOs provide 'democratic legitimacy' when they are involved in public policy processes that see citizens as central to solving community prob-lems,[8] they reduce the social isolation that leaves people vulnerable to xenophobic and racist appeals,[9] and they enhance public accountability and participation through opening up state adminis-tration to a democratically conceived 'citizen-based community'.[10] In other words, far from undermining democracy, there is widespread support for the view that the extra-parliamentary representative role that NGOs play when they act as advocates in public policy processes is, in fact, essential to a healthy democracy.

Other liberal democracies have recognised the benefits of a more engaged relationship between NGOs and governments. The attempts by the Australian Government to close down or marginalise all but the tamest NGOs stand in stark contrast to developments in the role of civil society in other liberal democ-racies, where frameworks for NGO–government relations are being built or rebuilt. In Canada, for example, the federal government and the NGO sector (called 'the voluntary sector' in Canada) have been working together to develop a partnership-based 'Accord'.[11] Similarly, in Britain the Blair Government has worked to develop a 'compact' with the voluntary sector there.[12] While these new arrangements are certainly not perfect—and critics remain on both sides of these relationships—they do at the very least constitute an acknowledgement of the essential contribution that the NGO sector makes to public policy and to democracy itself. They are a far cry from the approach that has been taken in Australia.

Governing for the mainstream?

In Australia, recent years have seen an unprecedented attack upon NGOs, most particularly upon those organisations that disagree with the current federal government's views and values. The attacks have come both from government itself and from close allies such as the Institute of Public Affairs. Questions have been raised about NGOs' representativeness, their accountability, their financing, their charitable status and their standing as policy advocates in a liberal democracy such as Australia.

The most public and visible attack on NGOs has been led by the right-wing Melbourne think tank, the Institute of Public Affairs (IPA), which first came to prominence in the 1980s when, backed mainly by the mining industry, it was instrumental in developing and promoting the policies of economic rationalism. The IPA now has close connections with the American Enterprise Institute, one of the principal sources of neo-conservative ideas that have so heavily influenced George Bush.

In the worldview of the IPA, NGOs are seen as 'selfish and self-serving' interest groups with little representative legitimacy. The vast store of knowledge of disadvantage and marginalisation held by NGOs is dismissed. Instead, they are seen as a group of professional stirrers who are not really interested in the welfare of those they claim to represent, but want only to feather their own nests, keeping their salaries and building their power bases.[13] This is a view largely informed by public choice theory.[14] In the public choice paradigm, actions such as policy advocacy, participation and consultation are to be avoided, as they are little more than a ruse designed to disguise the purely self-interested motives of the 'well-organised minorities'[15] who dominate Australian NGOs, and whose true motivation is really what is known disparagingly as 'rent-seeking', or the pursuit of additional funding and greater power and influence for their leadership.[16]

The IPA has been particularly critical of the legitimacy of NGOs in the policy-making process and has urged the federal government to withdraw financial support from NGOs that engage in advocacy. It argues that NGOs often 'invent' social and environmental problems and undermine the legitimacy of elected representatives in democratic states, referring to them as a 'tyranny of the minorities'.[17] Relying primarily on inflammatory rhetoric, the IPA has persisted with the argument that NGOs undermine the sovereignty of constitutional democracies, using pejorative descriptions of the NGO sector, such as 'the compassion industry', a 'dictatorship of the articulate' and a 'tyranny of the minorities', in its efforts to discredit the advocacy work of these groups.[18] Needless to say, this has not been well received by some charities. Oxfam has criticised the IPA's 'ongoing smear campaign against charities, welfare and aid agencies' and its 'ongoing vilification of organisations that campaign for human rights, corporate social responsibility and environmental protection'.[19] Nevertheless, in a recent publication on this issue the IPA has continued their call for greater regulation and restriction of the NGO sector.[20]

There is an uncomfortable match between the IPA's campaign against NGOs and the known views of Prime Minister Howard and several of his parliamentary colleagues. Prior to Howard's election in 1996 he outlined his view that there is a 'frustrated mainstream in Australia today which sees government decisions increasingly driven by the noisy, self-interested clamour of powerful vested interests with scant regard for the national interest'.[21]

More recently, in an address to the Menzies Research Centre, Howard repeated his pledge not to govern 'for the boutique interests of the few while ignoring the everyday concerns of the many', vowing that 'the politically articulate would not dominate at the expense of the unorganised mainstream of Australian society'.[22] It seems that both representing a minority and doing so in an organised manner are sins in the Prime Minister's eyes.

But the Prime Minister's public views do not always match his government's more covert behaviour. Other highly organised groups that are active in policy debates, notably business interests, escape the tests of 'mainstream representativeness' demanded of NGOs, despite the fact that they are clearly self-interested. Parliament House in Canberra is almost literally surrounded by expensive office buildings occupied by well-funded and highly effective business lobby groups. No one questions their right to exist and demands that they be made accountable to the community. A business minority is more acceptable to the Prime Minister than say a minority of community advocates, disability campaigners or environmentalists.

We now know from doctoral research by Guy Pearse that for a decade the Howard Government's climate change policies have been not so much influenced but actually written by a tiny cabal of powerful fossil-fuel lobbyists, self-described as the 'greenhouse mafia', representing the very corporations whose commercial interests would be affected by any move to reduce Australia's burgeoning greenhouse gas emissions.[23] This group consists of the executive directors of a handful of industry associations in the coal, oil, cement, aluminium, mining and electricity industries. Almost all of these industry lobbyists have been plucked from the senior ranks of the Australian Public Service, where they wrote briefs and cabinet submissions and advised ministers on energy policy. The members of the 'greenhouse mafia' claim to be more familiar with greenhouse policy than the government, because they are the ones who wrote it.

Several members of the mafia have rotated from one industry lobby group to another within the greenhouse network. As a result of the closeness of the personal and political connections within the network, Pearse concluded that the greenhouse mafia is probably the most potent lobbying alliance in Australia. Most of its members have been operating in Canberra for two decades, making their way up the bureaucratic ladder under Labor and Coalition governments. While Cabinet deliberations, ministerial committees and preparation of Cabinet submissions are meant to be confidential and beyond the reach of lobbyists—indeed, the unauthorised disclosure of Cabinet-in-confidence materials is a crime—the greenhouse mafia has 'unrivalled access' to internal government processes. Members of the greenhouse mafia even admit to being called in to government departments to vet and help write Cabinet submissions and ministerial briefings, referring to 'mutual trust' between the lobbyists and the bureaucrats (whose seats the lobbyists once warmed). 'It is about fixing the outcomes,' one said.[24]

But where Howard disingenuously talks of the 'mainstream' in his critique of NGOs, his colleagues are a little more transparent in their views of what is wrong with the advocacy work of these organisations. As the existence of the greenhouse mafia demonstrates, the problem is not influence per se, it is about *who* has influence and the sorts of values that inform their advocacy work. There is a clear agenda to restrict NGOs concerned with social justice, human rights or environmental protection. When these organisations step over an arbitrary, government-drawn line they become what Queensland Liberal Senator Brett Mason has called 'political wolves in charity sheep's clothing'.[25]

In the government view, such organisations must be constrained. In a 2005 speech to the Sydney Institute, Special Minister of State Eric Abetz proposed a new 'accountability regime' for charitable organisations that campaign on matters of policy. Abetz made special mention of the Wilderness Society and the RSPCA which, he claimed, 'were not only campaigning to influence the policies of the major parties [on forest policy and the banning of live exports, respectively], they were also effectively campaigning in favour of the ALP'.[26] The message to NGOs could not be clearer: if you're not with us, you're against us and we will make life hard for you.[27]

As these observations attest, the shifting relationship between NGOs and the federal government has not been driven solely by a different conception of the functioning of democracy. The relationship has been heavily influenced by the political objectives of the government. It is not NGOs as such that have been targeted but those NGOs that are seen to have an agenda that differs from that of the government. While there is a general view that NGOs have had too much influence and have too loud a voice in the public debate, certain NGOs have been spared criticism and threats, and indeed have been actively cultivated through increased public funding and the promotion of individuals to various government boards and bodies.

Taming strategies

While the World Wide Fund for Nature Australia (WWF Australia) appears to have had a close relationship with the Howard

Government since the 1996 election, the events surrounding the enactment of the *Environment Protection and Biodiversity Conservation Act 1999* (EPBC Act) were a turning point in this relationship. This Act brought wide-ranging and controversial changes to Commonwealth environmental laws. There was sharp disagreement among the larger environment groups about the merits of these legislative changes and debate about whether they should publicly support the Bill. The endorsements of the Act provided by WWF Australia—joined by three other smaller groups—contrasted with the often scathing criticisms made by opponents of the legislation, including the Australian Conservation Foundation (ACF), The Wilderness Society (TWS) and Greenpeace.

After the legislation was enacted, people associated with WWF Australia and the other supportive groups were appointed to serve on federal government environmental advisory committees. WWF Australia was also awarded a contract to disseminate information about the Act among environment NGOs. A report in 2004 concluded that WWF has enjoyed extensive financial support from the Howard Government, with a five-fold funding boost since 1996.[28] Total grants over the period amount to more than $15 million, with almost $20 million allocated since 1998–99, nearly all of it from the federal government. Funding to other environment groups, notably ACF and TWS (both of which were critical of the EPBC Act), has been slashed.

An analysis of the public statements made by WWF Australia and other environment organisations about the Howard Government's major environment policies shows WWF Australia's comments are mostly favourable, and sometimes highly complimentary, to the Howard Government. WWF Australia's statements reflect positions frequently at odds with those of other major environment groups, which are sometimes critical and sometimes supportive of Howard Government policies. WWF has also bestowed on the government several awards for its environmental achievements, including three Gift to the Earth awards, which the Environment minister displays on his office walls. In the course of the last election campaign WWF issued a joint media release with the government praising the latter's environmental achievements.

This history provides grounds for questioning whether WWF Australia can legitimately continue to describe itself as independent.[29] This perceived loss of independence is of considerable importance as it undermines WWF Australia's role in public debates about government policy and raises questions about whether it has misled its supporters and the general public. Because the public is justified in asking whether the opinions and activities of other groups are influenced by governments and businesses, the standing of all environment NGOs in the community could be jeopardised. It seems that WWF is being used by the Howard Government to endorse unpopular environment policies as the government often deploys WWF's name and statements in an effort to give credibility to controversial government policies. However, since Greg Bourne took over as chief executive of WWF Australia in 2004, there are signs that the organisation is taking a more independent stance, particularly on the issue of climate change.

A similar strategy of divide and rule has been applied by the Howard Government in the welfare sector. Organisations that have been critical of the government, such as ACOSS and the Brotherhood of St Lawrence, have been frozen out of debates and positions of influence. Others that have been friendly to the government have been favoured with funding, contracts and appointments of senior staff to various boards and inquiries. Two of the most favoured organisations have been the Salvation Army and Mission Australia. The rise in influence of the former CEO of Mission Australia, Patrick McClure, who played a prominent role in debates concerning the introduction of the GST that was in some respects counter to the position of other major welfare groups and more aligned with the government's position, is a case in point. McClure was subsequently appointed to head the government's review of the welfare system, which produced a report that became the blueprint for the Howard Government's controversial approach to welfare reform,[30] and is now a member of the government's Community Business Partnership. He was made an Officer of the Order of Australia in 2003.

The view from the NGOs

How do NGOs perceive this new and more hostile political environment? To answer this question, in 2004 the Australia Institute conducted a survey of Australian NGOs that include some advocacy in their role.[31] The survey explored how they get their messages out, their main audience, whether they are generally supportive or critical of government, barriers they face in being heard, their perceptions of government attitudes to debate, and whether they believe that dissenting views are welcomed or discouraged.

The web-based survey was sent to approximately 750 organisations that have some advocacy role. In total, there were 290 responses. The distribution of respondents by state and main field of activity was consistent with expectations, with the most important sectors being social justice and welfare (27 per cent of respondents), groups representing family, youth and older people (15 per cent), environment groups (12 per cent), human rights (11 per cent), disability and mental health (11 per cent) and women's organisations (9 per cent). While they cannot be named for confidentiality reasons, most of the largest and best-known NGOs responded to the survey, as did many small and medium-sized ones. The results provide a reasonably accurate reflection of the mix of views held by Australian NGOs that engage in advocacy.

Respondents were first asked whether they see themselves as supportive or critical of the federal government, and how this compares with the previous federal government. Not unexpectedly, NGOs are more likely to be critical than supportive of government policy—only 5 per cent say they often support federal government policy while 58 per cent say they are often critical. When asked to compare, respondents said that they are more likely to be support-ive of the previous rather than the current federal government. NGOs find the current federal government to be less sympathetic to their concerns than the previous federal Labor Government— 58 per cent say they are often critical of the current federal government while only 26 per cent say they were often critical of the previous government. This fact may explain why the Howard Government has adopted a range of strategies to silence NGOs. A similar though more muted pattern occurs at the state level.

When asked how successful they think they are in having their messages heard by government, there was a wide disparity among groups, depending in part on the area in which they work. Women's groups are the most likely to believe that their efforts are 'not at all successful' (43 per cent), with only one women's group believing that it has been highly successful. Groups represent-ing families and older people were the most likely to say that they are being heard by government, with 13 per cent reporting they are highly successful and only 6 per cent reporting no success.

Social justice and welfare groups are divided in their percep-tions of the willingness of governments to listen. These groups simultaneously report the equal highest percentage of respondents who believe that they are highly successful in having their message heard by government (13 per cent) and one of the highest pro-portions of respondents who believe they are not at all successful (28 per cent). There is evidence that this sector has been divided between those that have aligned themselves with the federal government (through, for example, accepting contracts to deliver services) and those that have remained more independent and critical.

The survey asked respondents to indicate the main barriers faced by NGOs in getting their message heard. While 38 per cent said that lack of media interest is 'often' or 'always' a problem, only 18 per cent believe that media indifference is 'rarely' or 'never' a barrier to getting their message heard. Three in five (61 per cent) said that the federal government is 'often' or 'always' not interested, with only 34 per cent saying the same about state governments.

Perhaps most disturbingly, the survey uncovered the extent to which governments use various methods to silence or intimidate its critics among NGOs. Clearly, any organisation that depends on government for funding gives government a hold over it. Among NGOs that receive government support, around 70 per cent report that their government funding at times restricts their ability to comment on government policy, although only

14 per cent say that this happens 'often' or 'always'. The results suggest that the more government funding an NGO receives, the more constrained it feels in making public criticisms. Some are required to consult the minister before making public comments, including having media releases vetted by the minister's office or the department. Others have been forced to remove from their publications and websites text seen to be critical of the government.

Many commented on implicit pressure to censor themselves. In the words of three:

> While not openly stated, it has been unequivocally conveyed that 'We do not fund organisations to criticise us'.

> The perception is that you toe the line or you risk getting defunded.

> It does have a chilling effect, however, wondering whether critical comment may ultimately affect our funding security.

Some make a conscious decision to avoid being compromised. As one wrote:

> We don't take government funding so we can criticise them.

And another:

> To have no government funding is liberating.

It is widely believed among NGOs that the federal government and, to a lesser extent, state governments want to silence public debate. When asked what they think the attitude of the

FIGURE 1: Attitudes of state and federal governments to debate (%)

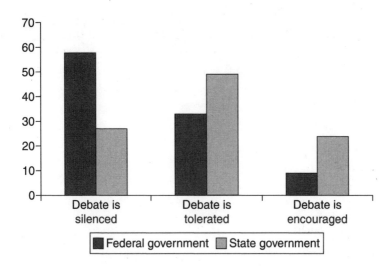

government is to debate in their area of interest only a small minority of respondents believes that debate is encouraged by the federal government (9 per cent), with 58 per cent believing that debate is silenced and 33 per cent believing it is tolerated (Figure 1). State governments are perceived less negatively, with around half believing that debate is tolerated and around a quarter each believing that debate is either encouraged or silenced.

Respondents were asked to express their agreement or disagreement with a number of statements about the role of dissenting voices in Australian public debate—see Table 1. Three quarters of respondents (76 per cent) disagreed with the statement that 'current Australian political culture encourages public debate', with one quarter disagreeing strongly.

TABLE 1: NGO perceptions of the role of difference and dissent in Australian public debate (%)

	Strongly disagree	Disagree	Agree	Strongly agree
Current Australian political culture encourages public debate.	25	51	20	3
NGOs are being pressured to amend their public statements to bring them in line with current government policy.	3	23	57	17
The Australian media provides a forum for a range of perspectives in public policy debates.	13	46	37	3
Individuals and organisations that dissent from current government policy are valued by the government as a part of a robust democracy.	42	50	6	2
Dissenting organisations and individuals risk having their government funding cut.	3	7	61	29

Similarly, 90 per cent of respondents believe that dissenting organisations risk having their funding cut. In the words of one:

> Peak bodies have had to tread very carefully in terms of retaining funding agreements during the Howard Government.

Three quarters (74 per cent) believe that NGOs are being pressured to make their public statements conform with government policy.

In addition to the threat of defunding, respondents identified several methods used by government to silence critics. As one respondent stated:

> It's done very cleverly—by selectively destroying organisations, defunding, public criticism, ministerial interference and criticism, excessive auditing and 'review'.

Management of consultation processes is something many NGOs are familiar with.

> It is clear from our funding contract with Government that it sees our role not as a peak body in a democratic society but as a mechanism to help the Government 'get its message out' and help the Government implement its policy objectives.

NGOs see the Howard Government as particularly skilful at using diversionary tactics.

> Government is very clever at pre-emptive announcements . . . Also clever at keeping the debate on its own terms through

public comment, question time in Parliament and denial of problems by consistently producing Government's record rather than considering what still needs to be done.

This perception of the diverse range of tactics adopted by governments is widely shared. In particular, many respondents singled out the way that the federal government seeks to undermine the reputation and challenge the credibility of its critics, something it does both publicly and privately. Denigration and public criticism is a commonly used method.

The Fed Govt strives to silence or weaken debate by Fed Govt ministers or parliamentarians openly denigrating certain sections of the community. This influences community opinions even though the community is not in possession of all of the facts.

Automatic visceral attacks on opinions counter to party line.

Persistent dismissal of contrary views by Government; attacks on the credibility of NGOs.

Bullying was referred to by quite a few.

Reactions to public comment are extreme . . . e.g. phone calls from senior staff keen to reduce further public debate.

Threats, bullying, personal attack unless debate is 'commissioned' by and 'controlled' by the Agency.

What next for NGOs?

As these survey results indicate, the threats to NGOs go far beyond empty political rhetoric. Since 2003 the government has escalated its attacks on the NGO sector through a range of strategies designed to restrict the advocacy capacity of the sector as a whole.

In 2003, the government commissioned the IPA to carry out an 'audit' of how NGOs relate to government departments. The government and the IPA kept quiet about the $50 000 contract until it was revealed in *The Age* newspaper in August of that year. This secrecy was ironic given the IPA's campaign for 'greater disclosure and accountability by NGOs receiving funding from and working with government agencies'.[32]

In the resulting report, titled *The Protocol: Managing Relations with NGOs*, the IPA expressed its concern that NGOs are provided with privileged access that distorts the functioning of democracy, arguing that: 'In many of their relationships with Departments, NGOs are granted privileges that are not available to members of the public. These privileges are primarily through the receipt of funding and the gaining of access.'[33] In light of what we know about government's close and secretive links with business lobbies such as the greenhouse mafia, these claims appear to be either naive or deliberately misleading.

The report recommended a 'protocol' for increasing scrutiny of the relationships between NGOs and government, using the language of transparency and accountability—as if, when left to their own devices, these organisations are bound to misbehave. The strategy is disingenuous: rather than focusing on *what* NGOs have to say to government, which may often be critical, the IPA focuses on *who* is speaking and *how* they are communicating, effectively shooting the messenger to avoid hearing the message.[34]

In a parallel strategy, also in 2003, Treasurer Peter Costello undertook to introduce a Charities Definition Bill that would disqualify charities that engaged in advocacy work, other than that which is ancillary and incidental to their main purpose. The threat was that, under the new definition provided in the Bill, lobbying or advocacy could result in the loss of an organisation's charitable tax status[35] or status as a deductible gift recipient (DGR). As many foundations can only donate to organisations that have DGR status (which makes the tax deductibility of donations possible), this could result in the indirect defunding of many such organisations. Although the government subsequently announced that it would abandon most of the draft Bill and would retain the common law definition of charity, many NGOs remain concerned that there will be a crackdown on their charitable status should they continue to engage in advocacy work.

These fears were strengthened by a draft tax ruling released in May 2005 in which the Australian Taxation Office (ATO) stated that '[p]olitical and lobbying purposes are not charitable. While such purposes may use educational means, this is not sufficient to show a charitable purpose', although the ATO did allow that 'political or lobbying activities that are merely incidental to a purpose that is otherwise charitable do not by themselves prevent that purpose being charitable'.[36]

Although the final decision may rest with the Australian Tax Office, it seems the process of implementing this regime will also be political. Early in 2005 Federal Minister for the Environment Ian Campbell wrote a letter to environmental NGOs that explicitly threatened to use the tax system to constrain their advocacy work. In the letter Campbell warned that organisations' tax-deductible status was dependent on their working on 'the conservation of the natural environment and not for any other purpose, such as political activity'.[37] It can be no accident that various entities of The Wilderness Society (TWS) were subject to three audits by the Australian Tax Office over the two years to the middle of 2006. None of them concerned the honesty of TWS's tax payments. They were entirely about the 'political' activities and charitable status of the environment group. The ATO found that TWS was entitled to maintain its charitable status but warned it about political activity. It would appear that the Howard Government is using the ATO to target its critics.

These continued attacks on the advocacy work of NGOs, along with the survey responses described above, paint a bleak picture of the state of public debate in Australia, suggesting a high degree of coercion on the part of Australian governments. Although frustration is expressed at state governments, it is apparent that the federal government is perceived by NGOs as being especially intolerant of dissenting voices. Many NGOs are reluctant, if not afraid, to speak out. While state governments are also guilty at times of pressuring NGOs to conform, the Howard Government's willingness to smother dissent poses a disproportionate threat to the democratic process in Australia.

As a result of these shifts many disadvantaged groups that had taken years to organise themselves sufficiently to have a voice have found themselves increasingly excluded from the policy-making process. It is not surprising to find that there has been a serious deterioration in relations between the federal government and NGOs in recent years, to the point where many believe they have been 'frozen out' and others fear they will have their funding withdrawn or tax status threatened.

The outcome for the broader Australian polity is that the knowledge and breadth of experience collected together in the NGO community are having much less influence on how we develop as a society than they should. Like individual citizens, community groups are being worn down and are increasingly reluctant to engage in the democratic process because they no longer believe that they can make a difference. At the same time, certain influential business lobbies have been brought into the fold, along with a few tame or uncritical NGOs like Mission Australia, the Salvation Army and WWF. There are grounds for serious concern that the longer this continues the more difficult it will be to reshape and rebuild the structures of democratic participation.

6

The media

Helen Ester

Chris Graham edits a national bi-weekly newspaper, the *National Indigenous Times*, a modest but politically robust publication with an audited circulation of around 10 000 and a website that averages about a million hits a month. It is published out of a newspaper office in the downstairs part of Chris Graham's house in suburban Canberra.

On the morning of 11 November 2004 Chris was feeling good about that week's edition of the paper as it contained exclusive and important information of government plans for the Aboriginal and Torres Strait Islander Commission (ATSIC). The leaked Cabinet documents were a classic journalist's jackpot of good, spin-free primary documents, full of facts, figures and unambiguous information about the government's plan to dismantle ATSIC, the first policy-making body to be elected by Indigenous Australians. But any reverie that morning was interrupted by unexpected visitors. Still in his pyjamas, Graham opened the door to two plain-clothes Australian Federal Police

(AFP) officers and noticed another three standing around in his driveway. Graham's partner was called out of bed. Neither was given time to change into day-wear, and while they were grilled and tape-recorded at the breakfast table strangers searched their bedroom, rifling through their clothes and private belongings and turning over the contents of their drawers and cupboards. A search warrant for the whole of the premises had been issued—even though the private upstairs home is obviously separated from the newspaper's office, the downstairs entrance of which is clearly sign-posted.

When Graham asked the police which Cabinet documents they were after—state or federal—his question was treated as impertinent, and although he took them straight to the Cabinet documents in question the search continued for a further two hours. Graham recalls that he,

> . . . gave the AFP the documents in the first half-hour. It wasn't hard, they were out on the desks downstairs . . . In any event the horse had bolted—the paper was already out. [But] the warrant was for the whole premises. The AFP scoured the entire newspaper office area, my backyard and my car and my partner's car, even though she does not work for the newspaper.[1]

In a related story also involving the *National Indigenous Times*, it was revealed in July 2006 that a public servant in the Howard Government's Office of Indigenous Policy Coordination (OIPC) had been suspended from her position for allegedly leaking information to the *Times*. Two days earlier the public servant's home had been raided by the AFP in search of documents allegedly leaked from the OIPC. The documents exposed a senior bureaucrat from the OIPC as posing as a youth worker on ABC Television's *Lateline* program and making explosive claims about paedophile rings in the Aboriginal community of Mutitjulu, apparently in support of similar unsubstantiated claims made by his minister, Mal Brough.[2]

These tales of the actions of the Australian Federal Police's so-called 'leak squad' are just two examples of the ways in which the Coalition Government is restricting the flow of information to the media. This chapter will look at the effect of these restrictions on political journalism by outlining the government strategies that are designed to disrupt, impede and direct the role of political journalists, particularly those based in the federal parliamentary press gallery.

Damming the flow of information

In spite of a media outcry at the time of the 11 November raid on the *National Indigenous Times*, the government is unrepentant about the obvious unfairness of picking on an independent media player with none of the protections available to the mainstream media organisations. In the end the police did not get what they really wanted from the raid—evidence to help track down the public servant who had leaked the documents. It was, however, evidence that the government's campaign to clamp down on leaks has created a climate of fear in the public service to deter them from leaking information to the media. Chris Graham believes that fear is now part of the Canberra political culture and he suggests that, 'It works. Many of my regular contacts are too scared to call'.

In interviews during 2003 and 2004, federal parliamentary

press gallery journalists also spoke of a fear factor. Michelle Grattan, political editor of *The Age* newspaper, said she had no doubt that the effect of high-profile police raids was to deliberately intimidate the public service. She claims that, 'The impact of this goes far beyond access for the media—they are intimidated generally, which has quite profound implications for policy'. Tony Walker, Grattan's then counterpart at the *Australian Financial Review*, said he found the public service was 'frightened' and that 'electronic surveillance, the ability to trace material and the penalties visited on people who leak' had ended the days when policy documents 'used to regularly fall off the back of trucks'. Geoff Kitney, then head of the *Sydney Morning Herald* Canberra bureau, suggested that public servants now found the prospect of briefing journalists 'quite scary', and that off-the-record briefings were no longer a standard way of cross-checking facts or following up information.

> Now when you call a bureaucrat they say: 'Sorry I can't talk to you', and refer you to the press secretary. There's a sort of reporting-back process, which allows the Government to monitor media inquiries.

Even journalists whose commentaries are often overtly pro-Howard, such as the political editor of *The Australian*, Denis Shanahan, pointed out that while tracking down leakers is not new, the public service was now 'much less open' because the system of hunting out and trying to stop leaks 'is much more efficient and ruthless now than it ever was'. Shanahan stressed:

> I'm not talking about people, you know, seeking you out to try and slip you the plans of an atomic reactor or something, I'm

talking about people willing to background you on a particular issue—they're just frightened to do it.

The political dividends of the fear factor also appear to outweigh its cost. In a 2005 debate over a disallowance motion regarding the Public Service Amendment Regulations, Opposition Senate Leader Kim Carr revealed that there have been,

> . . . close to 120 separate references to the Federal Police on what it [the Government] calls unauthorised disclosures. Through the leak squad some 32 000 staff hours have been spent trying to track down people who, the Government says, have broken their obligations in terms of revealing information. It has cost nearly $200 000. The number of people prosecuted can be counted on one hand.[3]

But the campaign does have political hazards for the government. This was made apparent in late 2005 after a senior public servant was charged under the *Commonwealth Crimes Act 1914* for allegedly leaking 'unauthorised' information. The case involved details of a Cabinet decision about war pensions that had found their way to Canberra press gallery journalists Gerard McManus and Michael Harvey, and subsequently into the pages of the Murdoch-owned Melbourne *Herald-Sun*. During the pre-trial proceedings against the public servant, journalists McManus and Harvey were called in as witnesses. But they refused to co-operate in spite of an offer of indemnity and would not name the person who leaked the Cabinet documents. Their defence—that the Journalists' Code of Ethics requires that they protect the identity of confidential sources—carried no weight and they were subsequently charged with contempt of court. Their trial was set down for October 2005, when they would face a maximum penalty of two years' jail.

The eventual outcome of the Harvey and McManus case reflects the intensity of the present government's anti-leaking campaign. The view that the journalists' plight was accidental (and politically embarrassing), 'collateral damage' holds some weight. Federal Secretary of the Media Entertainment and Arts Alliance (MEAA) Chris Warren described the charging of McManus and Harvey as 'a train wreck waiting to happen', because the Howard Government 'had clearly decided to crack down on leaked information' but failed to foresee that 'the inevitable consequence' of this is the jailing of journalists. The subsequent actions of Attorney-General Philip Ruddock suggested a government in damage-control mode. The week the McManus–Harvey trial was scheduled Ruddock suddenly intervened, asking the County Court of Victoria to reconsider and exercise its discretion to dismiss contempt of court charges against the *Herald-Sun* journalists. His submission 'expressed the Government's view that imprisonment would not be an appropriate penalty for the journalists'.[4]

The case placed the government's anti-leaking campaigns on the public agenda. At the time of the *Herald-Sun* journalists' case press gallery stalwart Laurie Oakes commented in a column on the Channel 9 website that in Australia,

> . . . it is the threat of leaks that keeps politicians honest . . . They are much more reluctant to lie or act improperly if they know they could be found out . . . A society where government has tight control of the flow of information—that is control of what the public is allowed to know—is not a democratic society.[5]

The need for this flow of information was also demonstrated in the case of *Bennett v President, Human Rights and Equal Opportunity Commission.* In this case Bennett, a public servant with the Australian Customs Service (but speaking in his position as president of the Customs Officers Association), made comments in the media about matters such as the proposed single Border Protection Agency. Bennett refused an order to stop talking to the media, even after he was charged under Regulation 7 (13) of the Public Service Regulations and subsequently suffered a salary cut and an enforced change in duties. Bennett challenged his treatment by taking his case to the Human Rights and Equal Opportunity Commission (HREOC). When the commission declined to investigate, Bennett challenged its decision in the Federal Court. During this case Justice Finn described the regulation as 'draconian', noting that such regulations were designed for a colonial era and were out of place in modern democracies where excessive government secrecy is a major issue. In Justice Finn's view, Regulation 7 (13),

> . . . impedes quite unreasonably the possible flow of information to the community—information which, without possibly prejudicing the interests of the Commonwealth, could only serve to enlarge the public's knowledge and understanding of the operation, practices and policies of executive government.[6]

Political journalism in Australian democracy

Many press gallery journalists saw the government's intensified anti-leaking campaign as part of a wide-reaching and deliberate media-management campaign to cut them off from a range of established sources of information. But complaints from journalists about access to information are neither new nor surprising. Michelle Grattan, who has worked in the gallery since 1970, said as much in the 2005 Deakin Lecture, 'Gatekeepers and Gatecrashers'.

> It is an old message that media and politicians are both natural adversaries and in a parasitic relationship. Their interests are often at odds. Sometimes they are openly at war, constantly they are engaged in a struggle of wits. What's interesting is how this traditional conflict and cooperation plays out in new circumstances.[7]

But does it matter to democracy? The specialist, critical expertise developed in the journalist round in the gallery is important to the media's role in a democracy. As Australian political scientist and media scholar Ian Ward has argued, 'Australia's democratic political life would be almost inconceivable without the news and interpretation provided by the media.'[8] Political journalists function as a kind of watchdog on the workings of parliament; a fulcrum in the see-saw between secrecy and transparency, between the fable and the necessity of a free press. The swings and roundabouts of this fourth estate[9] role are rarely visible except when information gets out that is in the public interest or when attempts are made to stop a story from running.

Freedom of the press is inextricably linked with the centuries-long evolution of Westminster-based democratic traditions. Journalists had to fight for the right to provide newspaper coverage of parliament, eventually (in the 1840s) winning the allocation of a separate physical space for the press inside the British Parliament.

This, according to media scholar Julieanne Schultz, was 'the moment after years of debate when the fourth estate became a place—in the form of a press "gallery"'.[10] In part because the early press fought for the right to publicise the activities of parliamentarians, core rights in modern representative democracies also came to pivot on notions of accountability and transparency—democracy has to be seen to be at work. Despite contemporary criticisms of the commercialism of much mass media, the role of political journalists and the public media in scrutinising and publicising the work of government is important to the democratic process.

Public sector media

Today the media's watchdog role in parliamentary democracies has largely defaulted to the press gallery round and to the public sector media. To a large extent, robust, agenda-setting public sector journalism has become a hallmark for free speech in modern democracies. In Australia, charters to uphold principles of editorial independence were legislated for the Australian Broadcasting Corporation (ABC) and Special Broadcasting Service (SBS). Although all federal governments (Coalition and Labor) have routinely cut funds and appointed political 'mates' to ABC and SBS management, the principle of editorial independence was largely stabilised over three decades. According to Schultz, from the 1970s on public sector media asserted and won 'increasing autonomy over content', and an 'uneasy truce' was maintained in the 1980s and into the 1990s.[11] During this time, for instance, a 1985 ABC brochure boasted of the vital importance of its independence from 'sectional interests' and about how it was a unique vehicle 'for innovative and reliable journalism'.[12] And in 1989 the federal government ended the uncertainty of annual budgets by agreeing to fund the ABC for three-year periods. During these decades a serious threat to the otherwise 'hands-off' approach occurred once in 1991, during the Gulf War, when Labor Prime Minister Bob Hawke intervened over the amount of air time given to war critic and Middle East expert Dr Robert Springborg, and was mollified when the ABC equalised time with alternate commentators.

It was not until the first year of the Howard Government that the decades-long 'uneasy truce' started to come undone. During the 1996 federal campaign Howard targeted 'political correctness', and ABC programs addressing issues such 'multiculturalism, reconciliation, anti-discrimination and environmentalism'.[13] Once in office, the government cut funding by $55 million and instituted a national review of the ABC, chaired by businessman Bob Mansfield. The subsequent report from the review recommended ways to economise the activities of the ABC, including the controversial (but short-lived) shutdown of Radio Australia. The most unexpected outcome of the Mansfield review, however, was the outpouring of public support for the ABC that manifested in 10 000 submissions from the public.

By the time of Australia's controversial involvement in the war in Iraq any hands-off role by the executive had all but disappeared. The then Communications minister, Senator Richard Alston, ordered extensive surveillance of ABC reporting. The broadcasts of current affairs and news journalists were not only monitored for balance, but also for bias in voice intonation and emphasis. As a result of this year-long 'bias-watch' the minister put 68 alleged incidences to the ABC's Complaints Review Executive. Only two were upheld. Dissatisfied with this, Alston put the complaints to a specially convened Independent Complaints Review Panel and then to the Australian Broadcasting Authority (ABA), and another fifteen were upheld. In the aftermath of this, in 2005 Margaret Simons wrote that 'at every stage, the review bodies confirmed the majority of coverage was even-handed'.[14] But two years later the professionalism of ABC journalists again came into question—and was all the more demoralising for being instigated from the inside, this time by Managing Director Russell Balding. In the lead-up to the 2004 federal election Balding hired external media monitors Rehame to trawl for 'bias and balance' in political coverage. ABC staff were once again vindicated when Rehame found a difference in coverage of the parties of only 1.1 per cent, in the Coalition's favour.

But practical outcomes do not appear to have been the aim of these exercises. The main effect of Alston/Balding 'bias-watch' campaigns, and even the earlier Mansfield review, has been the creation of fear and uncertainty among ABC staff. Seasoned ABC reporter Quentin Dempster describes these actions as 'political bullying and internal buckling' that undermine staff morale.[15] Simons found 'there is a new awareness of weighing words and tone of voice', and one senior broadcaster confirmed that staff felt bullied by the bias-watch exercises.[16] Dempster warns, 'there is danger, already apparent to many, that the ABC's journalism is degenerating into careful blandness'.[17]

Views from the gallery

Michelle Grattan (*The Age*) is emphatic about the importance of context over content in the age-old struggle between governments and gallery. Grattan illustrated how changes to the way this is played out have a direct impact on political journalists' capacity to be effective information 'gatekeepers' and 'gatecrashers'. In 2003 and 2004 there were signs of fundamental changes to the terms of this engagement. This was made apparent in a series of interviews with 24 mostly senior journalists from all mediums.[18] The interviews highlighted issues such as control and surveillance, and paint a picture of cumulative deterioration in sources of political news and information, describing new layers of disempowerment, frustration and disinformation. Most of the interviewees noted that the Howard Government had ushered in a decade of unprecedented executive control over political communication. Rob Chalmers (*Inside Canberra*), who has witnessed governments come and go over five decades, went so far as to describe Howard as a 'control freak'. Louise Dodson, then head of bureau of *The Age* newspaper, said there was a dearth of 'usable research information from the public service', and that the decline started almost from the first day of the Howard Government.

> There was much easier access under the Keating and Hawke governments. Now, public servants have told me, even departmental heads have told me, that in 1996, just after the Howard Government got in, they had been rung up and told to report all calls by journalists to the Prime Minister's press office.

The Prime Minster's office oversees media management policy, including the appointments of ministerial media officers. According to Michelle Grattan these are 'very carefully, centrally vetted these days'. Grattan has also found that she now has to deal with 'unprecedented numbers of press secretaries and gatekeepers'. Her then counterpart on the *Australian Financial Review*, Tony Walker, also regarded the control exercised by the Prime Minister's personal office as 'a particular feature of the Howard Government'. Kerry-Anne Walshe from the *Sun-Herald* described an 'octopus-like' network of media control extending from the Prime Minister's office to ministerial press secretaries, departmental press officers and electorate media officers. Ross Peake (*Canberra Times*) said the greatest challenge of the past five years was working up against a new 'barrage of press secretaries'.

The gallery responses beg the question of how the Coalition Government's apparently larger, more influential network of ministerial media advisers differs from their Labor predecessors', particularly Labor's taxpayer-funded National Media Liaison Service (NMLS nicknamed 'aNiMaLS'). Richard Griffiths (*Capital Monitor*) noted that in 1983 Labor had set up 'Animals' and a media service in every capital city for rapid government responses to media questions, and that it took about 'four or five years for the service to turn into a propaganda arm'. But he says that after the first Howard Government fulfilled a 1996 election promise to disband Labor's NMLS it was replaced with a ministerial media unit.

> They were going to save lots of money and lots of staff, and no minister, apart from the Prime Minister, would have a press secretary and everyone would share journalists to write their press releases for them. That lasted for all of about a year and then all the ministers started to get their own staff together, and [now] they're falling out of the doors down there to try and fit them in.

Tony Walker (*Australian Financial Review*) remembered that NMLS had mainly directed resources to getting 'the government's spin throughout the media', but argues that in comparison the reconstituted media management network does much more than this. Walker claims that the Coalition has been 'the most controlling [Australian] government' he has 'ever come across', because,

> ... [the government] not only have totally unhelpful press secretaries, but they have got people to watch press secretaries to make sure that the same message is being put out by everyone—every minister, every back bencher. The result is that there is practically no information outside the government line. To eke out anything of any consequence you have to be in the gallery for a fairly long while and know people other than these spin doctors, or to have a particular relationship to handle them.

Jim Middleton (ABC TV) also saw the increased size and professionalisation of the Coalition's brand of political media management as less sophisticated than the previous government, but more successful. 'It's cruder but more effective. The key is simply the withdrawal of access—that's the most significant difference.'

Disinformation and distrust

In 2001 the gallery–media officer relationship reached an all-time low when journalists found they had been deliberately used by ministerial media minders to help spread lies in the 'children overboard' affair. This controversy erupted after it became clear that misleading photographs had been handed out to the press. These were used to back false claims by the Prime Minister and the then minister for Defence, Peter Reith, that some members of a boatload of asylum seekers had thrown their children overboard in a desperate bid to head off interception by the Australian Navy.

In an unprecedented move, the federal parliamentary press gallery committee endorsed a formal submission from nine journalists to the subsequent Senate inquiry into a 'Certain Maritime Incident', tabled on 13 May 2002. It is a strongly worded protest about the dangers of distributing 'clearly false information', and describes how this led to 'widespread resentment among journalists'. The introduction said:

> A government campaign of censorship and misinformation, which peaked during the *Tampa* incident and continued through the HMAS *Adelaide* 'children overboard' affair, is unprecedented in recent times. It involved the Ministries of Defence and Immigration as well as the office of the Prime Minister.
>
> However, the high level of deliberate deception—which came clearly to light in Senate Estimates committee hearings—could not have been perpetrated without the involvement of senior and junior public servants.
>
> As well as fostering feelings of distrust and resentment in the Federal Parliamentary Press Gallery, this affair has underscored an urgent requirement for safeguards and guidelines to avoid a repeat of such blatant political manipulation of the bureaucracy.[19]

Head of the *Canberra Times* bureau Ross Peake said disinformation experienced during the 'children overboard' incident led the gallery to 'totally re-examine what officials say to us and put it through a different filter'. Filters include not only re-evaluating assumptions about ministerial media officers but also long-standing conventions about ministerial accountability. Between October and November 2002 false information was repeated by the Prime Minister and the Defence Minister, and was allowed to stay on the public record even though ministerial officers and some senior public service personnel knew the story was untrue.

Howard and his ministers later claimed they did not lie because they were not advised of the truth. From this, journalists learnt they could not assume ministerial 'spokespeople' were by default an extension of the minister, or that information to and from ministerial staff was known and endorsed by the minister. False presumptions about ministerial accountability also undermines the routine checking of facts through covert or overt confirmation by ministerial advisers, or ministers themselves. Patrick Weller's analysis of the children overboard incident argues that the 'fundamental question' raised by this affair 'is one of accountability'. Journalists must now ask:

> Are ministers 'informed' if they are given a heavily qualified warning, or must it be explicit and in writing before they regard themselves as being advised? Can they choose not to be informed, so that they have a level of 'deniability' and can plead innocence?[20]

Press conferences

The blocking and distortion of information by ministerial staff is one of several other more routine changes mentioned by gallery journalists. The two most prominent are the decline of 'all-in' press conferences and the ascendancy of talkback radio as a primary tool for directly communicating with the public about policy decisions and policy issues.

Under the Coalition Government, press conferences have become highly controlled and professionally stage-managed events. Former editor of the *Canberra Times*, Jack Waterford, told the ABC Radio National's *Media Report* that at times the gallery had bought a 'pathetic bargain'. For example:

> The Prime Minister will stride up in front of a lectern, say about five or six sentences and then walk away, answering no questions whatever, or giving only trivial answers to them. That's not submitting yourself to the scrutiny of the public.

Karen Middleton (then with the *West Australian*) described a launch-release-unveil formula where 'these days, so much is staged . . . There is much [over] emphasis on launching and releasing and unveiling . . . it's all organised in advance'. Alison Carabine (2UE/Southern Cross Network radio) says that the faux informal doorstop conferences are not much better.

> First of all you get the same old suspects day in, day out, and the ones you normally really want to talk to don't make themselves available. Secondly, you don't get new stories as you are simply getting reaction . . . We've got bulletins every hour,

every half-hour in breakfast shows and . . . in so much [of our] content we are forever filing reaction.

Political journalists' access to the executive is significantly diminished by the demise of all-in press conferences, creating much resentment among reporters. And John Howard's influence is being felt around the world. In May 2006, when newly elected Canadian Prime Minister Stephen Harper adopted Howard's strategy of staged conferences, the Canadian press gallery called a strike in protest.

Talkback radio

Politicians have for years favoured commercial talkback radio as an effective means of talking directly to the public and avoiding difficult or 'pesky' questions from the journalists. Under Howard, talkback radio has really come into its own, in part thanks to the groundwork laid by the Hawke Labor Government when it amended media regulations to allow radio stations to 'aggregate' into networks. The most visible effect was the disappearance of 'radio alley' (a section of the gallery where there were eighteen different commercial radio stations). Just two bureaus remain—the Macquarie and Southern Cross networks. It is well known that Howard's favourite host is Macquarie Network's Sydney-based Alan Jones. To reach the rest of the nation the Prime Minister need only visit one other gallery bureau, the Southern Cross Network. Who needs the gallery when you can talk to millions of voters in two sessions of friendly talkback hosts and moderated calls from the public?

This has put the Southern Cross Network's gallery bureau in the box seat. Alison Carabine heads the two-journalist bureau, and described how the Prime Minister has a 'savvy' way of fulfilling all daily media obligations in one go, through a half-hour interview with Southern Cross radio host Neil Mitchell (3AW). Howard uses talkback as a 'three in one' because a television crew always records the session and the radio audio is transcribed. So 'print and radio all feed off the one interview', and so do TV and radio 'as the interview goes to air live so there is no editing'. Where once journalists would speak of 'sound grabs', it is now common to hear talk of 'pic grabs' (TV) and 'text grabs'.

The high value Howard places on talkback as a prime media strategy is illustrated by the following anecdote from Alison Carabine.

One day when I was setting the PM up in the studio for the interview something exploded in the panel and smoke wafted up. Now it was my immediate reaction that we wouldn't do the interview in the studio and we should do it on the phone. But the Prime Minister disagreed, he just wanted to go ahead. The reason why he was so determined is because these interviews are always filmed by Channel 9 and get beamed out to the rest of the gallery, the Prime Minister's press office produces a transcript so everyone in the gallery gets it—and from there everyone in the entire country accesses this interview. The Prime Minister knew that if he didn't do it on camera that day, he would have to hold a press conference and [all] the television bureaus would be able to cover it. This way [using studio talkback radio] the gallery radio bureaus get the audio they need, newspapers get the transcript and television

get the in-studio vision. In other circumstances, to get television cover you would have to do a press conference or a
doorstop.

Ross Peake (*Canberra Times*) sees this strategy as 'press conference by radio', and expresses his frustration that follow-up phone
calls to the minister's office for clarification are a waste of time
because, 'You're told to read the transcript—you get absolutely
nothing at all'. The result is that government-distributed talkback
transcripts are most often the source of the day for political quotes
and information. Ian McPhedran, head of the News Ltd bureau,
pointed out that 'on any given day you might get four of five
interview transcripts', but that attempts to follow these up with
further questions always hit a dead end with ministerial press
officers because 'they direct you [back] to the transcript'.

Political reporting based on government-distributed transcripts is also a cause for concern to Glenn Milne (then with
television's 7 Network). Transcript information 'is not news at all'.
Milne argues that talkback radio hosts are regarded as 'personali-
ties' rather than journalists, and it seemed to him that often radio
hosts only set out to 'show their audience that they have influence
and success rather than pursuing the stories or accountability'.
Rob Chalmers (*Inside Canberra*) agrees, pointing to the style of
prominent talkback host John Laws:

> . . . if you ever read the transcript he's hopeless because [Laws
> is] . . . not a journalist and he doesn't understand the issues. In
> fact he has said, 'I'm not a journalist, I'm an entertainer'. One-
> on-one any decent politician can defeat some bloke that's
> running a talkback show.

For Chalmers, relying on transcripts from talkback is neither news nor journalism.

The chief political correspondent for the *Daily Telegraph* (and gallery president at the time of the interview), Malcolm Farr, summarised the pre-eminent position of talkback this way:

> The main difference under Howard has been the proportion of time given to the gallery. Hawke did not give a lot of formal access, but did provide a lot of informal information. Howard's routine is to cover all bases, Brisbane, Sydney, Melbourne, Adelaide and Perth. This avoids the informed receptors of the press gallery . . . It is awful to see journalists captive to transcripts. Journalists shouldn't be waiting round for transcripts; the PM should be reacting to journalists, not the other way round.

The gallery journalists also suggest that Howard's three-in-one strategy and tight media control have diminished other democratic institutions, including the parliament itself. Parliamentarians are naturally in the media shadow of their leadership, but according to Geoff Kitney, then head of bureau of the *Sydney Morning Herald*, under Howard the spotlight is more often on the Prime Minister himself and away from his ministerial colleagues because 'the big decisions come from his office and the group around him'. Rob Chalmers (*Inside Canberra*) described Parliament House as becoming increasingly like a 'taxpayer-funded television studio for the Prime Minister', and was outraged when he witnessed Howard choose a media conference to tell Australians of the government's decision to go to war in Iraq and only inform the parliament several hours later. To Chalmers this was a flagrant disregard of the parliament. Ross Peake (*Canberra Times*) observed that although prime ministers characteristically do not like 'doing that old fashioned thing' of making a statement to parliament, with Howard 'the push is to get into the public forum'.

Conclusion

In 2006 the Howard Government showed an increasing disregard for the role of robust political journalism in Australian democracy. In quick succession the morale of journalists and other staff at the ABC was dealt a double blow. With the advantage of a majority in both Houses of parliament, the government amended the ABC Act to specifically remove the board position of a staff-elected director. In June the government reminded Aboriginal Australians of its distaste for 'politically correct' journalistic content by appointing Keith Windschuttle to the ABC Board to join two other directors who vigorously challenge Aboriginal and historical accounts of the extent and manner of Indigenous dispossession. And in July the ABC Board (on spurious commercial grounds) reneged on its commission to publish a biography of Howard supporter Alan Jones, even though it was researched and written by senior and respected ABC investigative journalist Chris Masters.

It may be that the next generation of political journalists will find it hard to withstand the pressures of modern-day government media management and manipulation. Today's senior journalists talked about a hollowing-out of the gallery's expertise and pointed to the rapid turnover of young people in the 135 to 140 or so mainstream gallery journalists. Tony Wright (*Bulletin* magazine) detected the beginnings of this trend in 1989.

When I first came here in 1989 it was probably the end of that era where journalists would have killed to come to Canberra to report the big picture, to report federal politics. These days there is a small group of people who have been here for a very long time. They have the corporate memory that was once held by quite a lot more people, or a higher proportion of people. This is followed by a slightly smaller group, who have been here as long as I have, or a bit longer. Then there is a great gap to the majority of people who come here as young journalists . . . They will spend a year or two, or even less, here, and then head off and be replaced.

The 'old guard' in the gallery is clearly concerned about the changing rules of engagement between political journalists and the government. Their perspectives show that the last decade has seen an increased focus on strategies to block and control access to information flows from the gaze and analysis of the critical expertise of journalists in the parliamentary round. The trend to devalue and avoid the critical expertise of the press gallery does not bode well for the future of political journalism in the federal parliamentary round, nor for public knowledge about the deliberative processes of policy-making in the parliament and the accountability of the executive.

7

The public service

Geoffrey Barker

Old public servants still relish the confrontation between Prime Minister Gough Whitlam and his Treasury secretary, Frederick Wheeler. The best version has Whitlam imperiously asking Wheeler after a meeting, 'Why are you still in my office?' Wheeler, unflinching, replies between clenched teeth, 'Because I have things to tell you, Prime Minister, ignorance of which could bring down your government.' Then there is the legendary exchange between Prime Minister Malcolm Fraser and Defence Department Secretary Tony Ayers. 'I don't want to hear that,' Fraser reportedly said in response to some bad news from Ayers. Ayers's reply (expletives deleted) was, 'I'm not here to tell you what you want to hear. I'm here to tell you what you need to hear'.

That's how it was when the mandarins ruled, when, for better or for worse, secretaries were permanent and powerful and did not hesitate to stand up to their political masters. In those days politicians protected and defended key democratic institutions like the public service, ensuring they were in cautious, expert and reliable hands.

A week after John Howard came to office in 1996 he sacked six of the nation's eighteen public service department secretaries, the top-level administrative heads of government departments. They had done nothing wrong or disloyal; Howard just didn't want them. A month later he ousted Dr Mike Keating, head of the Prime Minister's department and titular head of the APS. Howard replaced Keating (no relation to Paul) with Max 'the Axe' Moore Wilton, who assumed with relish the role of Howard's chief bureaucratic enforcer until his resignation in 2002 to become chairman and CEO of the Sydney Airport Corporation.

For the Australian Public Service, the Coalition Government's coming to office was deeply troubling. The Prime Minister's sackings underlined the Coalition's desire to reduce the size and transform the culture of the Australian Public Service (APS). The Coalition wanted a lean private-sector machine applying business principles to public policy administration. The public service was expected to become responsive to the Coalition's political agenda, which included the sale of remaining government business enterprises and the outsourcing and downsizing of many public service functions. 'Previous incoming governments said, "Don't be against us",' a former secretary remarked to the writer. 'This government asks, "Are you one of us?"'

In the eleventh year of the Howard Government, the Coalition's transformation of the public service is considerably advanced. There was a 21 per cent cut in public service numbers from 1996 to 2000 (from 143 218 to 113 561) but numbers have since climbed back to 131 396 (an overall reduction of 8.3 per cent in the decade). In addition, the employment of large numbers of consultants in departments has substantially boosted numbers on the public payroll.[1]

More than previous governments, the Coalition has moved to ensure that its people and its values dominate the federal administration. Its appointees are entrenched in the courts, the bureaucracy, the diplomatic service and across the vast spectrum of advisory boards, commissions and authorities through which much government power is exercised. Some top public service jobs—including some departmental secretaries—are now filled by political appointees.[2]

The numbers and role of private ministerial and other government staff advisers have expanded substantially, to more than 520 at last count.[3] Advisers occupy key positions as ministerial minders, gatekeepers and enforcers, ensuring that public servants know what ministers want and give it to them. But they are entirely unaccountable to parliament, and are subject to no legislated norms of conduct. Some advisers seem to have the specific role of keeping certain information away from their ministers so that the ministers can evade responsibility, claiming that they were not told and did not know about matters that might prove damaging to the government.

Advisers are usually party political allies of ministers, and often ambitious to become parliamentarians themselves. Their primary task is to advance the minister's agenda and interests. Departmental liaison officers (DLOs), drawn from the public service, are supposed to remain apolitical coordinators of ministerial–departmental relations, but the boundaries between the roles of advisers and DLOs inevitably become blurred. These developments have spawned arguments about whether, or to what extent, the Howard Government has 'politicised' the public service.

Australian expert on public sector accountability Richard

Mulgan has argued that the extent of politicisation 'should not be exaggerated', but concludes a study of the issue with the observation:

> Politicisation of the APS, in the sense of appointments to suit the preferences of the government of the day, has been gradually increasing over recent decades. The process has been given added impetus by the growing insecurity of tenure among secretaries and by the sometimes uncritical adoption of private sector management models.[4]

By contrast Dr Peter Shergold, the current secretary of the Department of the Prime Minister and Cabinet, dismisses any suggestion of politicisation as 'a product of conspiratorial imagination ... a cop-out'. Shergold says: 'Public servants, it is suggested, now willingly do what governments require of them because they are politicised. In fact they do it because they remain steadfastly apolitical. They would do it for any government.' In the same speech Dr Shergold had sufficient good humour to add '... but then I would say that, wouldn't I?' Of course he would.[5]

So where lies the truth? What has the Howard Government done to the public service? This chapter will argue that while the Howard Government has done little that was not started by earlier, and usually Labor governments, it has imposed its will more deeply and more broadly than earlier governments. It will also argue, however, that politicisation of the public service is less significant and less troubling than the pervasive climate of uncertainty, fear and retribution created by the expanding army of ministerial advisers who seek to manipulate even low-level public servants for openly partisan purposes.

The importance of an apolitical public service

Australia still has a recognisably Westminster-type public service, largely appointed and promoted on the basis of credentials, neutrality and expertise. But it increasingly displays attributes of a Washington-type public service, where politically appointed or politically sympathetic advisers occupy key positions. A major and disturbing difference, however, is that the Australian system lacks the public checks and balances that help to protect the US system. The lack of checks and balances has become increasingly apparent since the Coalition Government won control of the Senate in 2005 and ordered public servants not to give evidence before Senate estimates hearings, one of the key national accountability mechanisms. So Australia arguably is getting the worst of Westminster and Washington—neutral expertise without power and political power without accountability.

To the extent that this shift is occurring it is threatening the healthy functioning of Australian democracy. It compromises the provision of frank and objective advice to ministers by enabling political advisers to put pressure on public servants to shape, skew and manipulate advice to suit ministerial political agendas. Given the understandable reluctance of public servants to risk penalties (including jail) for revealing how advice has been manipulated, the shift corrupts truth and openness in government and makes it easier for governments to seek public support for policies on the basis of false or selective information that suits their political purposes. The overall result is a gradual debauching of the independent, albeit responsive, public service as political operatives acquire increasing administrative power.

Notwithstanding Dr Shergold's spirited defence of the public service as 'a far better place than I joined twenty years ago', and his insistence that it 'must be both apolitical and politically responsive',[6] there is no shortage of evidence that the Coalition Government has been and remains willing to ride roughshod over the constitutional roles and independence of key democratic institutions, including the public service, the courts and the military high command. As power has been increasingly centralised in the Prime Minister's office, this tendency has been revealed dramatically in events including the so-called 'children overboard' affair, the government's decision to go to war in Iraq on the basis of false intelligence, the destruction of the Commonwealth Employment Service and Employment National, and the Australian Wheat Board (AWB) kickbacks scandal.

Next we consider the climate of uncertainty and fear now evident across the public service before examining some case studies which reveal the impact of the transformed public service on accountability.

Fear and uncertainty in the public service

The Public Service Commission's 2004–05 *State of the Service* report[7] reveals that, in the eleventh year of the Howard Government, a climate of profound uncertainty, if not fear, pervades much of the Australian Public Service.[8] The uncertainty is the result of two factors: first, increasing demands made on public servants by ministerial advisers; second, the lack of clarity about how those demands ought to be met by a bureaucracy that is supposed to be at once 'apolitical' and 'responsive to the government'.

Noting that its APS employee survey showed that 'one in five public servants had direct contact with ministers and/or their advisers during the past 12 months', the report said that up to 65 per cent of employees were not sure whether their agency had protocols in place to guide interactions with ministers' offices. The report further suggests that, 'This level of uncertainty is disturbing, especially regarding the protocol requiring oral briefing to ministers or ministers' staff on key issues is confirmed in writing'.[9]

So concerned was the Public Service Commission that in March 2006 it published what it called 'a guide to official conduct for APS employees and agency heads', setting out the responsibilities of public servants and delineating the difference between the political role of advisers and apolitical role of public servants. Whether the new guide will help resolve uncertainties remains to be seen. In the *State of the Service* report the commission quoted an unnamed respondent as saying, 'You can have all of the protocols you want, but if the minister's office wants something you give it to them . . . In previous jobs I had been told . . . not to put things on e-mail so there was no record of it'.[10]

The demands now made by political advisers on public servants to provide information to support the political dimensions of policy agendas is an insidious manifestation of what seems a sustained campaign by the Howard Government to keep the public service afraid, off-balance, and uncertain about the balance between being apolitical and being responsive, between giving the government frank and fearless advice and complying with what it wants.

Public servants who have expressed views or acted in ways displeasing to the government have been subject to various forms of pressure, discipline and vilification. The government has shown itself willing to spend hundreds of thousands of dollars to keep public servants in line. Two high-profile examples stand out.

Shortly before the 2001 election the Navy chief, Vice-Admiral David Shackleton, flatly contradicted government claims that asylum seekers had thrown children into the sea. He came under immediate pressure to recant and issued a statement saying: 'My comments in no way contradict the minister. I confirm the minister was advised that Defence believed children had been thrown overboard.'[11] His careful words spoke of what Defence believed rather than what the Navy knew to be the case. But they allowed the government to perpetuate the children overboard falsehood until polling day, and showed the entire public service what could happen to even senior military figures who dared to contradict the government.

In early 2004, Federal Police Chief Mick Keelty told a TV interviewer that if the Madrid terrorist bombing was linked to Spain's involvement in Iraq then no one could guarantee that something similar would not happen in Australia.[12] It was a self-evident, even trite, observation, but it appeared to contradict Prime Minister Howard's claim that Australia's involvement in Iraq had not increased the terrorist threat to the country. Keelty came under immediate and immense pressure from Howard and other ministers, gratuitously supported by the then Defence Force chief, General Peter Cosgrove. He was forced to issue a humiliat-ing 'clarification' saying his remarks had been 'taken out of context'. They hadn't been, but the episode was widely interpreted as a government move to ensure unquestioning bureaucratic adherence to the Howard line on Iraq.

This is in addition to the determination the government has shown in initiating police investigations into disclosures of information it wanted kept secret, as discussed in the previous chapter. More subtly, but not less importantly, the cutting of public service jobs and the growth in consultant numbers have devastated skills, experience and institutional memory in many departments. The departments are thus arguably far less capable of resisting the demands of political advisers than they might otherwise have been.

It is, of course, true that after thirteen years in opposition the Coalition came to office to find the public service strongly pre-disposed to Labor's approach to public policy. Yet the Coalition has paid a price for the ill-disguised hostility with which it has imposed its will and its ways on the public service. The result, as Verona Burgess has noted,[13] is that 'the bureaucracy's reputation has been stained by political scandals and controversies' that include the waterfront dispute, the IT outsourcing debacle and the fire sale of government property, the children overboard affair, failed oversight of the collapsing insurer HIH, huge expenditure on government advertising, regional rorts, the immigration and asylum-seeker debacles and the AWB kickbacks case. Looming over all of these matters was the decision to go to war in Iraq on the basis of false intelligence and with little apparent independent input from Defence, Foreign Affairs or any other agency that might have urged caution about what has become a dangerous long-term military commitment.

To quote again from the *State of the Service* report:

> There will inevitably be situations in which employees are uncertain about how to respond to a minister or an adviser . . . Employees faced with difficult situations, and inexperienced employees, need to be able to discuss the problem without fear with more senior managers and/or a central area of expertise

and support, rather than be left to make decisions on their own and feel isolated.[14]

It is, of course, in the government's interest that individual public servants are left uncertain and isolated: they are more likely to comply without question.

The Public Service Commission's focus on this issue suggests that it sees it as the key issue threatening the apolitical character of the public service as it faces demands to be responsive to the government. As the public service commissioner, Lynelle Briggs, asked when launching a good-practice guide for public servants, 'What do you do when a ministerial staffer is screaming at you down the phone to recommend a particular project, or when they are adamant that you should recommend funding for a project because the minister "really wants" to fund it?'[15]

Two case studies

The 'children overboard' affair

The so-called 'children overboard' affair in October 2001 was a particularly egregious example of the political manipulation of the public service, the aggressively expanding role of ministerial advisers and the limits to parliament's ability to check executive government power. Detailed treatments of the issue are to be found in the report of the Senate Select Committee on a Certain Maritime Incident[16] and in *Dark Victory* by David Marr and Marian Wilkinson.[17]

In the heated political climate of a federal election campaign dominated by national security and border protection issues,

Minister for Immigration Philip Ruddock announced on 7 October 2001 that a number of children had been thrown overboard from a 'Suspected Illegal Entry Vessel' intercepted by HMAS *Adelaide* off north-western Western Australia. The story was repeated throughout the election campaign by other senior ministers, including Defence Minister Peter Reith and Prime Minister John Howard, to support their campaign argument that Australia needed to take a tough stance against 'illegal' (and undesirable) arrivals seeking political asylum. Photographs purporting to show children thrown overboard were released to the media. But the story was untrue; no children had been thrown overboard.

Although doubts about the 'children overboard' claim were circulating among naval officers and defence civilians within days of Ruddock's original false claim, no correction, retraction or expression of uncertainty was made by any federal government minister before the election on 10 November 2001. On 7 November, three days before the election, the then acting chief of the Defence Force, Air Marshal Angus Houston, told Reith that children had not been thrown overboard.[18]

Subsequent attempts by a Senate committee to investigate the affair were significantly frustrated by a Cabinet decision to 'fence off' ministerial and prime ministerial staff from the reach of the inquiry by refusing access to prime ministerial staff and to public servants working in ministerial offices at the time. Nevertheless the non-government committee majority concluded that several factors contributed to the children overboard story being circulated and uncorrected. These included 'genuine miscommunication or misunderstanding, inattention, avoidance of responsibility, a public service culture of responsiveness and over-responsiveness to the political needs of the minister, and deliberate deception motivated by political expedience'.[19]

The committee found that Minister Reith, who refused three formal requests to give evidence, 'deceived the Australian people'.[20] It was also critical of senior public servants and military officers, including Jane Halton, then chair of the People Smuggling Task Force (subsequently promoted to become secretary of the Department of Health and Ageing), the then chief of the Defence Force, Admiral Chris Barrie, and the then secretary of the Department of Defence, Dr Alan Hawke.

The committee noted particularly what it called 'a serious accountability vacuum at the level of ministers' offices'.

> There now exists a group of people on the public payroll—ministerial advisers—who seem willing and able on their own initiative, to intervene in public administration, and to take decisions affecting the performance of agencies, without being publicly accountable for those interventions, decisions and actions.[21]

The report identified 'haranguing interventions'[22] of Reith's ministerial staff into the Department of Defence, and their failure to 'adequately assess and give proper weight to advice from the department'.[23] The report said Reith's media adviser, Ross Hampton, seemed 'agitated and quite angry at times' as he pressed Defence officials for information.[24]

As things turned out, the government was returned to office. The importance of the children overboard story in shaping the election outcome remains uncertain. The children overboard issue exposed the extent of government pressure on uniformed and civilian defence and intelligence officials to support the false story told by Ruddock on over-hasty advice from public servants seeking to be 'responsive'. It reveals the uncertainty and fear of military and civilian personnel being harangued by ministerial advisers. And it reveals the inability of the Senate inquiry process to question and hold ministerial minders and department liaison officers accountable for their conduct.

The AWB Iraq kickbacks scandal

The federal government's handling of the Australian Wheat Board (AWB Ltd) oil-for-food scandal reveals how relations between ministers, their advisers and public servants are manipulated to enable ministers to sidestep responsibility for their actions (or lack of action).

Simply stated, the scandal involved AWB's payment of some $300 million in kickbacks to the Iraq regime of Saddam Hussein in defiance of United Nations sanctions against Saddam's regime. The Australian Government was legally responsible for ensuring that Australian firms complied with the sanctions. It manifestly failed to do so, apparently preferring to maximise gains for Australian wheat farmers in the Iraq market rather than to abide by its international legal obligations. Even as the Australian Government was preparing for war against Iraq, it was turning a blind eye to AWB Ltd, helping to fund the enemy by breaking sanctions through the kickbacks scam.

As the Clerk of the Senate, Harry Evans, has observed, the scandal might not have been disclosed without pressure from the United States Congress and from the United Nations investigation conducted by Paul Volker, a former chair of the US Federal Reserve Board.[25] Once it did come to light John Howard ordered public servants not to give evidence to Senate estimates hearings, a move subsequently condemned as unlawful by Evans. Instead the government set up the Cole commission of inquiry with carefully crafted terms of reference to investigate the scandal. This had the effect of taking the issue away from the primary political accountability mechanism of Senate estimates and handing it instead to a legal forum limited by its formal terms of reference.

What quickly emerged from Cole's inquiries was evidence in the form of 21 cables dating from early 2000 from the Australian Permanent Mission to the United Nations, warning ministers and senior public servants of allegations that AWB had been involved in 'irregular payment methods'.[26] A 2003 report prepared for the Coalition Provisional Authority in Iraq by a US Army captain, Blake Puckett, claimed that every wheat contract had included a kickback to Saddam's regime of between 10 and 19 per cent. Ministers defended their inaction by dismissing the claims as allegations by trade competitors designed to discredit Australia, insisting that AWB, formerly a government body, was a company of high repute. Australia's UN Mission was described as a post box that rubber-stamped AWB deals with Saddam's regime.[27]

Reading the cables from the Australian Mission in New York leaves no doubt that the diplomats there were fully alert to concerns over the allegations of kickbacks, and that they were regularly informing ministers and their bureaucratic colleagues. But evidence given to Cole by ministerial advisers and ministers tells another story, a story of people apparently determined to minimise the potentially damaging advice from carefully protected ministerial political redoubts.

Innes Willox, chief of staff to Foreign Affairs Minister Alexander Downer, told the Cole commission that the minister relied on his six advisers to determine which cables to bring to his attention. A short daily 25-page summary of cables would be prepared by the department and sent to the minister. Whether or not he read the summary would depend on time constraints and other events.[28] Downer, despite pleading memory loss on some issues, confirmed he often did not read the summaries. He said he did not read a January 2000 cable warning that AWB could be paying kickbacks because he was on leave and because the contents were not sufficiently urgent. He did not note Captain Puckett's findings because Puckett was a junior officer.[29]

John Howard and Trade Minister Mark Vaile offered similar explanations. Howard said he would not have expected the January 2000 cable to be brought to his attention 'in the context of the time' because there was no belief within the government that the AWB was other than a company of high repute.[30] In evidence, Vaile repeatedly said he could not answer questions and that he did not know why his department did not bring the kickbacks to his attention.[31] Both Vaile and Downer said they had confidence in their departments, with Downer saying his department did a good job and faithfully implemented government policy.

But what was the policy? To comply with UN sanctions? Or to prevent competitors from taking Australia's wheat market in Iraq? To do both would be extremely difficult and the actions of some bureaucrats appear to reflect their anxiety to avoid possibly acting in ways contrary to the government's essentially inconsistent goals.

Robert Bowker, head of the Department of Foreign Affairs and Trade (DFAT) Middle East branch, responded to a warning cable by telephoning an AWB official, who told him, 'This is bullshit'. That response satisfied Bowker and he took no further action. Jane Drake-Brockman, then a DFAT assistant secretary, signed a letter which she said she did not draft, telling AWB that DFAT saw 'no reason from an international legal perspective' why it should not enter a commercial arrangement with a Jordanian trucking company to deliver Australian wheat to Iraq.[32]

The effect of their actions was to help perpetuate a scam about which the government had been warned in detail in cables from the Australian United Nations Mission. Whether or not Bowker and Drake-Brockman could have been more attentive to the cabled warnings, it seems they were straining to do what they assumed the government wanted them to do; that is, to ensure that wheat exports were maintained by not examining too closely AWB's actions. They were, arguably, normal risk-averse public servants trying to be responsive to the government.

For the public service more broadly, the performances of Bowker and Drake-Brockman, and other public servants who also ignored the cabled warnings, imply the emergence of a culture of covering your arse while you keep your head down. To get along, you go along. You don't make waves. You respond without question. That is a consequence of the Coalition's management of the public service.

Historical background

Like the Whitlam Government in 1972, the Howard Government came to office committed to far-reaching economic and social change. Ironically, it was changes introduced by the Whitlam Government and the later Hawke and Keating Labor governments in 1984 and 1994 that helped clear the ground for Howard's sustained push to impose the Coalition's style and values on the public service.

Before the election of the Whitlam Government there had been no independent and wide-ranging inquiry into government administration for more than 50 years.[33] Lacking administrative experience, the incoming government was heavily influenced by Dr Peter Wilenski, who came into government as Whitlam's private secretary and was appointed special adviser to the Royal Commission on Australian Government Administration chaired by Dr H.C. Nugget Coombs, arguably Australia's pre-eminent senior bureaucrat at the time. The Whitlam Government's primary concern was the power of the permanent heads of federal departments, the conservative and long-entrenched mandarins who ran their departments as feudal fiefdoms, resisting, in Labor's view, its program for social reform and equity. Whitlam, like Howard, wanted less of the mandarin culture and more of a managerialist culture. It was under Whitlam that political staffers, or 'minders', were first appointed to ministers' offices.[34] The goal of the Coombs Royal Commission was to make the public service 'more responsive to government, more efficient and effective and with greater community participation'.[35] As Briggs says, 'Coombs has been a catalyst for and has strongly influenced public sector reforms since that time'.[36]

In 1984 the Hawke Government pushed public service re-form further with its Public Service Reform Bill and the associated Members of Parliament (Staff) Bill. The former renamed depart-mental permanent heads as secretaries and introduced fixed-term (generally five-year) appointments designed to create mobility through the rotation of secretaries around departments. The latter

Bill set out conditions governing the employment of the staff of ministers, party leaders, senators and members as well as ministerial consultants. Significantly, though, it said nothing about their roles and responsibilities, and created no framework for their accountability.[37]

Ten years later, in 1994, the Keating Government introduced legislation to enable persons from outside the public service to be taken on as department secretaries for fixed terms and to allow secretaries to trade their public service tenure for terms of up to five years and salary loadings initially of around 20 per cent. The legislation was supported by the then Liberal opposition on the ground that it 'gives the government some flexibility in the types of people it may wish to appoint as permanent heads of departments'.[38]

It was against this background of Labor Government legislation that the newly elected Howard Government was able to oust six of the eighteen departmental secretaries, and the secretary of the Department of Prime Minister and Cabinet. It was also able to recruit outsiders to head departments, including the ill-fated Paul Barratt, former Business Council chief executive, who was installed as Defence Department secretary; Mark Paterson, former head of the Australian Chamber of Commerce and Industry, who is now head of the Department of Industry, Tourism and Resources; Peter Boxall, who became Finance Department secretary after serving as Peter Costello's chief of staff; and Michael L'Estrange, former executive director of the Menzies Research Centre, who is now head of the Department of Foreign Affairs and Trade.

In his 1997 Garran Oration John Howard reiterated his commitment to a 'non-partisan and professional public service', and said he opposed any trend toward the US-style of political appointments to the higher bureaucratic levels. But he also said the government wanted in the top leadership of the public service 'people who it believes can best give administrative effect to the policies which it was elected to implement'.[39] This declaration seemed tantamount to an assertion of the government's right to hire and fire secretaries on the basis of their perceived enthusiasm for the government's political agenda.

The messy 1999 sacking of Defence Department Secretary Paul Barratt by Defence Minister John Moore resulted in a further strengthening of the government's power over the public service. Barratt, who had been head-hunted by Howard from the Business Council of Australia, appealed against his sacking, but a subsequent Federal Court decision confirmed that secretaries could be terminated at the pleasure of a minister provided the minister gave reasons, and that 'loss of trust and confidence' was sufficient reason. It was a judgement to concentrate the mind of every senior bureaucrat who might have been tempted to occasional dissent.

In 1999 the Howard Government overhauled the Public Service Act, incorporating a statement of values and a code of conduct into the legislation. The values statement declares the public service 'apolitical, performing its functions in an impartial and professional manner'. It also declares the APS 'responsive to the government in providing frank, honest, comprehensive, accurate and timely advice and in implementing the government's policies and programs'.[40] The code of conduct requires public servants, among other things, to 'behave honestly and with integrity'.[41]

The initial legislation was fiercely opposed by Labor on the ground that it 'would have led to a public service which would have been too susceptible to pressures from the government of the day and less willing to offer critical advice'.[42] Labor moved more than 50 amendments, which the government resisted, and the stalled legislation became a double-dissolution trigger. But compromises were eventually negotiated and the legislation was modified and passed with Labor support.

The 1999 overhaul also made significant changes to the Members of Parliament (Staff) Act, but none of the changes related to accountability issues or mirrored the public service and parliamentary service reforms. No rules, it seems, bind minders to norms of conduct.[43]

For public servants it is a fine balance to be at once apolitical and responsive. Doing so under the pressure of demands from unaccountable ministerial staffers might, at times, be impossible. Certainly it would seem particularly onerous when, as Briggs says, ministerial staffers are shouting political demands down the phone. A climate of uncertainty, even fear, in the public service arguably suits the government. It strengthens the ability of ministers and staffers to get public servants to do their political bidding while evading accountability for their actions.

A key paragraph in the Public Service Commission's guide to official conduct for APS employees and agency heads says:

Ministerial employees provide important guidance about the minister's policy and requirements and, by so doing, help APS employees to be responsive. However, they cannot direct APS employees. In forging good relationships with ministerial employees, APS employees need to recognise their different roles and responsibilities. Ministerial employees have a political role to help the minister fulfil his or her aims across the portfolio. APS employees are responsible to the minister through the Agency head and have an apolitical role to help the minister draw on the depth of knowledge and experience in the APS, provide a longer-term perspective, and ensure due process under the law.[44]

That, at least, is the way things are supposed to work, according to the commission's guide. The reality, as its 2004–05 *State of the Service* report shows, is different. The report notes that while two thirds of public servants in direct contact with ministers or advisers were highly or very highly confident that they could balance being apolitical and responsive, nearly one third had only moderate or low levels of confidence.[45]

Commenting on the low levels of awareness about the existence of protocols for dealing with ministerial staff, noted above, the report says it should be a priority for the APS to put further effort into promulgating and actively supporting policies or protocols on public servants' interactions with ministers and their offices. An unnamed public servant is quoted in the report as saying:

> Advisers are political and often want to amend briefing to give it a political slant. Holding a good line against advisers' requests to compromise 'frank and fearless' advice depends more than anything on SES [the Senior Executive Service] being prepared to sign off on good quality briefs and resist pressure to compromise.[46]

But whether or not protocols are in place, and whether or not public servants are aware of them, the reality for public servants is that their relationships with ministerial advisers are ultimately heavily weighted in favour of the advisers. Public servants are bound by the values and the code of conduct; advisers are under no such constraints. Public servants can be held publicly accountable for their actions; advisers are not subject to external accountability mechanisms. Public servants are supposed to serve long-term national interests; advisers openly serve the short-term political interests of their political masters. Public service is regarded as a career, even a vocation; being a ministerial adviser is a temporary billet for people with political, business or possibly academic ambitions, a job where knowledge, skills and contacts for other more lucrative work are accumulated. Public servants are supposed to be policy experts; advisers are openly political operators. In these circumstances, in the daily rough and tumble of politics and administration, individual public servants or agency heads concerned about their jobs and career prospects are understandably uneasy about saying 'No' to determined advisers acting on behalf of powerful ministers.

The government's destruction of Employment National, the government agency that replaced the former Commonwealth Employment Service, demonstrated these realities. The affair involved the loss of millions of dollars and thousands of jobs, and the sacking by then Finance Minister John Fahey of two Employment National boards (one of them composed of public servants) which refused to sign a $100 million contract they regarded as commercially unviable.

The government wanted to hand the provision of employment services to favoured church and charitable agencies, and to private companies that were located at the rate of about four to one in Coalition-held regional electorates rather than Labor-held electorates.

The then secretary of the Department of Employment and Workplace Relations, Dr Peter Shergold, complained to the Press Council about reports on the issue in the *Sydney Morning Herald*. The Press Council finding was that the newspaper should have sought greater balance in its articles by seeking earlier comment from Dr Shergold. But most significantly it found the newspaper was justified in its suspicions about political interference and that the department's role in some aspects of the process 'would lead to the conclusion that the department was in some way party to the tainted outcome'.[47]

Under the Howard Government these trends have intensified as the role and numbers of unaccountable ministerial staff have continued to expand. From modest beginnings under Whitlam, the number of ministerial advisers grew progressively larger during the Fraser, Hawke and Keating years. In a major study of ministerial staff for the Federal Parliamentary Library, Ian Holland noted concerns that 'staffers' lack of accountability sits uneasily with both their power and their public position. 'Put most simply', Holland wrote, 'if ministerial staffers are more than merely their bosses' ciphers—and the general view is that they are—then their actions must be more transparent than is currently the case'.[48] He proposed the calling of staffers as witnesses to parliamentary committees on a similar basis to the appearance of public servants, the insertion of conduct clauses into the act governing ministerial staffers, transparency of ministerial staff contracts and parliamentary regulation of numbers and/or conditions of employment of ministerial staff. This is unlikely to happen. Neither the government nor the opposition has any interest in diminishing the role now occupied by advisers. Both understand the value of advisers in leaning on public servants.

Conclusion

The Coalition Government has clearly had a dramatic impact on the public service over the last decade. From its highest to its humblest echelons the public service has been remade to ensure its compliance with the government's political agenda. With honourable (and often modest) exceptions, the fearless permanent mandarins of the past have been largely replaced by cautious transient managers, some of whom are open government allies. Some senior posts are occupied by people whose abilities may be beyond doubt, but who owe what they are and have to government patronage. At lower levels an expanding phalanx of private political advisers has interposed itself between the public service and ministers to ensure that the will of the government is not frustrated by inconvenient advice. There have been administrative scandals but undoubted political successes. At the same time public accountability mechanisms have been progressively compromised as ministerial advisers have increasingly reached down into the lower levels of the public service to achieve their aims. While advisers increasingly exercise power without responsibility, public servants have little choice but to succumb.

8

Statutory authorities

Andrew Macintosh

A key theme of the Howard Government's four terms in office has been the centralisation of power. This has involved drawing powers away from the states and territories towards the Commonwealth, illustrated most vividly in 2005 with the changes to the industrial relations system. Within the federal government, the object of the centralisation agenda has been to gather power around the Prime Minister's office and Cabinet. Much of the debate about this issue has concentrated on the government's attempts to undermine the independence of the public sector and the diminishing role of parliament, especially parliamentary committees. However, of equal importance has been the reduction of the independence of non-departmental public agencies.

Defining non-departmental public agencies (hereafter referred to as public agencies) is not as easy as it may seem. At the most basic level, the federal government can be broken into three parts: the legislature, the executive and the judiciary. Public agencies straddle the judiciary and the executive.[1] While departmental agencies are under the direct control of, and are responsible to, government ministers, public agencies are, to some extent, operationally separate from ministers and Cabinet. Control is usually left to one or more non-ministerial persons (for example, a CEO, judge, or board) who is granted powers to act under legislation or by government decree. The heads of the organisations are generally answerable to a minister, but there is an operational divide that provides the entities with some scope for taking actions without political interference.

There are many different types of public agencies. Some are regulators, others run businesses, while there are also institutions like the Australian Broadcasting Corporation (ABC) that provide services directly to the community. In addition, there are judicial and quasi-judicial bodies, along with many agencies whose functions are solely advisory that are supposed to ensure that ministers and departments receive external or expert advice.

There are various reasons for establishing these entities, although independence is usually a crucial part of their raison d'être. At some point it has been decided that the functions of the entity would be performed more effectively if they were vested in an agency that is separate from related departments and the responsible minister. This can be a product of the fact that the objectives of the organisation are believed to transcend the partisan interests of the government of the day. The ABC, for example, is often seen as performing an essential service to democracy such that it needs to be shielded from government meddling. Similarly, cultural and artistic institutions like the National Gallery and National Museum are supposed to reflect national values and ideals rather than the views and opinions of a particular political party. As governance scholar Roger Wettenhall has argued, organisations like these were established in recognition of the need to distinguish between 'what is governmental and what is truly national'.[2]

Without independence, the reason for the existence of these organisations is often lost or, at the very least, greatly diminished. For example, a partisan national broadcaster is more a vehicle for propaganda than a facilitator of democratic processes. Regulators that are too close to governments are often biased and frequently fail to achieve their objectives because of inconsistencies in the way they enforce legislative requirements. And there is little point in having advisory committees and 'independent inquiries' if they only provide information that the government wants to hear. In short, when agencies lose their independence, they can also lose their public value and can easily become a hindrance to democratic processes.

The Howard Government's approach to public agencies

Public agencies can create difficulties for governments because their independence allows them to engage in activities that may conflict with the interests of their political masters. Such clashes between the government and public agencies are healthy. In many cases they provide a vivid illustration of why independent agencies are established. Put simply, the political demands of government can sometimes obstruct due process and the provision of public services.

The Howard Government has gone to great lengths to prevent public agencies from acting in ways that are inconsistent with its own political and ideological objectives. To stifle independence and dissent among these organisations, two main tactics have been employed. The first has been the systematic stacking of the boards of public agencies. This has involved both selective appointments and the removal of independent and dissenting voices from positions of authority. Most, if not all, Australian governments have been guilty at some stage of making politically motivated appointments to public boards. The unique aspect of the Howard Government, however, has been both the scale on which it has occurred and how it has been achieved.

According to insiders, before John Howard even became prime minister a list had been developed that identified people within public institutions that needed to be removed to advance the cause of the conservatives. In 2002, respected journalist Andrew Clark wrote the following in the *Australian Financial Review*:

> In 1995, after Howard regained the Liberal Party leadership, he held meetings with close associates in the party, business and various institutes. The message was simple: the key to returning Australia to a nation unsullied by Labor's years was the trashing of the reputations, followed by removal, of targeted people in the public service, academia, ABC and the High Court.
>
> And there was a list. It may have changed from time to time, but for participants at these secret meetings there was unanimity about the targets. A single-minded, but never declared, pursuit of this list has contributed significantly to the unusual atmosphere surrounding the Government.[3]

Since coming to office, the Howard Government has purged public agencies of dissenters and those viewed as being sympathetic to opposition parties, while also ensuring that a large proportion of the people appointed to public boards have links to the Coalition or a commitment to conservative political ideals. The Prime Minister's office apparently now vets all senior appointments to public agencies, making balanced representation difficult to achieve.[4]

The second strategy used by the Howard Government to enhance its control of public agencies has been to strip back their powers and institutional independence. A considerable amount of this restructuring has occurred as part of a review triggered by the 2003 Uhrig Report,[5] which examined the governance arrangements of statutory authorities and public office holders. The report was undertaken after extensive lobbying by the business sector and was prepared by businessman John Uhrig who, at the time of the inquiry, was chair of the mining giant Santos Ltd. After a largely internal review process, he handed down a report containing recommendations that, according to Wettenhall, 'were in line with, and helped give form to, the Howard Government's own thinking'.[6] That thinking was based on the notion that ministers should have complete control over the activities of public agencies unless those agencies are engaged in a commercial operation or there is some other exceptional circumstance warranting independence. Theoretically, this approach is justified on the grounds of financial accountability and the principle of responsible government, which suggests that the executive is responsible to ministers who are then responsible to parliament. Given the fact that ministers are responsible to parliament, they must have the capacity to dictate how agencies are managed; or so the argument goes.

There are several flaws in this argument, including the fact that the constitutional conventions governing ministerial responsibility are now seldom followed. There was a spate of ministerial resignations for conflicts of interest and misconduct in the first couple of years of the Howard Government, but there have been none for over seven years despite numerous breaches of the Prime Minister's ministerial code of conduct.[7] Resurrecting hierarchical lines of accountability from agencies to ministers to parliament is futile unless the government is willing to hold its ministers responsible for their failures. And turning away from ministerial control does not mean there must be a void in accountability. Institutions like parliamentary committees, the Auditor-General and the Commonwealth Ombudsman have proven to be quite capable of ensuring that the activities of public agencies are appropriately monitored. There is no reason why these alternative forms of accountability could not be continued and improved without any need for greater ministerial interference in the activities of many non-departmental bodies.

Another flaw in the government's arguments for greater control of public agencies is that many of these bodies are of little value if they lose their independence. When the division between ministers and public agencies is eroded, their capacity to perform their public functions can be greatly reduced. This is not always the case; there are instances where the governance arrangements of public agencies can be rationalised without any significant loss in effectiveness. However, the government is trying to apply the logic behind the Uhrig Report across the majority of public agencies in a manner that indicates that there is more at stake than merely accountability and ministerial responsibility.

The evidence suggests that the real reason for the structural changes that have been made to many agencies is the government's desire to concentrate power, stamp out dissenters and reshape Australian society in accordance with conservative ideals. This was implied in a letter from the Prime Minister to ministers dated 29 November 1996 that was leaked to the media in early 1997. The letter stated that the Department of the Prime Minister and Cabinet was reviewing how to 'make greater use of provisions enabling the Government to direct statutory authorities . . . in the performance of their functions'.[8] It also said that ministers 'need to be conscious of the extent to which the establishment of these bodies limits governments' own sphere of control and constrains the options available to them'. The Prime Minister went on to say that 'he wanted the freedom to act without legislation' and, in a pointer to the board stacking that would follow, he said that he planned to increase his power to terminate appointments to statutory agencies.

Some examples

Examples of how the Howard Government's agenda has affected the operation and independence of public agencies are everywhere, although the stacking of the ABC is among the best known.

The ABC

Sources within the Liberal Party have been reported as saying that 'as far as Liberals go, the major cultural war of the last 20 years has been against the left of the ABC'.[9] To execute this war, the Howard Government turned first to Donald McDonald, a long-time friend of the Prime Minister whose wife is also reportedly a close friend of Janette Howard. At the time of his appointment, McDonald had strong ties to the Liberals and had extensive experience in artistic and cultural enterprises. However, as Ken Inglis, a historian of the ABC, has noted, McDonald has proven to be far more independent than many may have first anticipated,[10] so much so that his reappointment in 2001 was opposed by a number of Coalition members who resented his lack of progress in 'reforming' the ABC. At the time of writing, there was considerable speculation about his future, which was not quelled by the announcement in June 2006 that his term had been extended for a further six months only. It has been reported that he is 'hated and detested' within federal Cabinet for his failure to confront the perceived left-wing bias within the ABC and his involvement in the departure of Jonathan Shier from his post as managing director in 2001.[11]

Although McDonald may have failed to stick rigidly to the government's plan, there have been numerous other ABC appointees over the past ten years who have been more compliant. Michael Kroger, former Victorian Liberal Party president and long-time Liberal powerbroker, was appointed to the ABC Board in the late 1990s. During his time on the board he left little doubt about his intentions. In an interview on radio station 3AW in 2002, he stated:

> I've complained at board meetings—probably at every meeting for the last 4 years—about things that happen within the corporation and it pains me to say it publicly . . . but essentially the Newscaff [news and current affairs] that comes out of the ABC in Sydney I think it lacks diversity, I don't think it's balanced and unfortunately I have to say so in these circumstances.[12]

Inglis has written that Kroger believes that 'the board's role is straightforwardly political'.[13] This claim is supported by Kroger's declaration that he had a 'statutory duty' as a board member to inform the public that the ABC was not balanced, as well as his insistence on intervening in editorial matters.[14] For example, in 2002, he told the producer of *Four Corners* that any story on his friend Alan Jones should be 'overwhelmingly positive'.[15]

While Kroger was on the board of the ABC, he was accompanied by Ross McLean, who was the federal Liberal member for Perth between 1975 and 1983, and Judith Sloan, a conservative labour market economist with links to the Centre for Independent Studies, a right-wing think tank, and the H.R. Nicholls Society. Leith Boully, who was appointed in 2000, was also a former member of the Northern Territory Young Country Liberal Party,[16] while Maurice Newman, who served on the board between 2000 and 2004, is known to be a close confidant of the Prime Minister.[17]

The current board includes conservative columnist for *The Australian* and vocal ABC critic, Janet Albrechtsen, and former News Ltd columnist Ron Brunton. Brunton used to be the director of the Indigenous Issues Unit at the Institute of Public Affairs (a right-wing think tank), and he has played a central role in a number of the Howard Government's cultural and ideological battles. He is an anthropologist by training and he first attracted public attention when he questioned the religious beliefs of the Jawoyn people, which were central to the Coronation Hill land rights claim.[18] After that, he gained a reputation as a greenhouse sceptic and right-wing commentator on Indigenous issues, notwithstanding the fact that he apparently 'has not undertaken any sustained or systematic fieldwork in an Aboriginal community and has no basis for claiming ethnographic authority in relation to any recognised Aboriginal group'.[19]

Brunton's reputation as a critic of Indigenous causes is well earned. His targets have included the Royal Commission into Aboriginal Deaths in Custody,[20] the Mabo High Court case[21] and Sir Ronald Wilson's *Bringing Them Home* report on the stolen generations, which he described as 'one of the most intellectually and morally irresponsible official documents produced in recent years'.[22] Brunton was also a key player in the Hindmarsh Island affair, as he, along with fellow News Ltd columnists Christopher Pearson and Piers Ackerman, publicly challenged the validity of the notion of 'secret women's business'.[23] In various News Ltd newspapers, he described the claims concerning sacred sites as 'fraudulent', 'totally fabricated'[24] and 'a cynical attempt to manipulate Aboriginal tradition to prevent the construction of the bridge'.[25]

The suggestion that the secret women's business was a hoax was initially supported by the 1995 report of the South Australian Liberal Government's Hindmarsh Island Bridge Royal Commission. However, in 2001 the Federal Court found that the allegations that the secret women's business had been fabricated were unsubstantiated.[26] In his decision, Justice von Doussa was critical of the Royal Commission and a number of those who questioned the validity of the secret knowledge, including Dr Philip Clarke and Dr Philip Jones (who was later appointed to an inquiry into the National Museum). At the time the claims of secret women's business were first made Clarke and Jones held positions at the South Australian Museum, and they subsequently played an important role in shaping the outcome of the Royal Commission. They also appeared as witnesses for the developers in the Federal Court case.

Justice von Doussa was scathing of Clarke, describing his denial of the secret women's business as a 'spontaneous assessment' that was reached within hours of learning of the original declaration and before he had read all of the relevant material. He said that Clarke's 'diaries show that he was the originator of the fabrication theory, and that he thereafter embarked on a course to undermine and discredit' those who were supportive of the existence of the secret knowledge. Justice von Doussa concluded by saying that Clarke's role in the Royal Commission lacked 'professional objectivity and was inappropriate', that he had 'serious concerns about the objectivity of Dr Clarke and the opinions he has given in evidence'.

Brunton and Albrechtsen are joined on the ABC Board by Steven Skala, who was a director at the Centre for Independent Studies, and John Gallagher, who has been described as a 'conservative Queen's Counsel'.[27] In mid-June 2006, the government also announced the appointment of Keith Windschuttle and Peter Hurley to the board, both for five-year terms. Windschuttle was previously a Marxist and was a member of the Labor Party between 1969 and 1991.[28] In the late 1970s and early 1980s, he called for 'public ownership of the means of production' and argued that 'we need to maintain a viable alternative press and an independent broadcasting system'.[29] Since then he has lurched to the right, and is now known mostly for his involvement in the cultural wars due to his criticism of the ABC and the part he has played in disputes over colonial history and the depiction of frontier conflicts at the National Museum, which is discussed below.

Peter Hurley has been described as a 'prominent South Australian publican'.[30] He heads the South Australian-based Hurley Hotel Group, is the senior vice president of the national branch of the Australian Hotels Association (AHA) and is the president of the South Australian branch of the AHA. But it is not Hurley's apparent lack of broadcasting experience that has raised eyebrows. He, along with companies he is associated with, have made donations to the Liberal Party and Liberal Party front groups like the Free Enterprise Foundation, and he has been described as a 'Liberal powerbroker',[31] a label he claims is inaccurate.[32]

The appointment of Windschuttle and Hurley came soon after the announcement of the government's decision to abolish the position of staff-elected director. This followed disputes on the board between the last staff-elected director, Ramona Koval, and several Howard Government appointees.

The stacking of the ABC has not been confined to the non-executive directors of the board. Despite the fact that the managing director is a board appointment, there is little doubt that the government played an active role in the appointment of Jonathan Shier as managing director in 2000. Paul Daley, writing in the *Bulletin*, said that Shier was 'appointed from relative obscurity in March 2000 with a specific mandate to attack the culture at the ABC'.[33] His political credentials for the job were impeccable, having previously been president of the Victorian Young Liberals and an adviser to a federal Liberal minister. According to reports, Shier went about trying to rid the ABC of its perceived bias and, in doing so, alienated many people both inside and outside the organisation. Donald McDonald is said to have decided with his fellow board members that Shier had to be replaced, yet Shier resigned before he was pushed, only twenty months after he was first appointed.

He was replaced by Russell Balding who, by all accounts, performed his role admirably under trying circumstances. In early

2006 he resigned from his post and his position was filled by Mark Scott, a former editorial director at Fairfax who reportedly has solid political connections, which may stem from his time as a staffer with the former New South Wales Liberal minister for Education, Terry Metherell. When the appointment was first announced people questioned whether Scott had the broadcasting and managerial experience to perform the job.[34] The ever-colourful conservative commentator, Padraic McGuinness, described Scott as lacking in 'journalistic experience' and suggested that he would not take on the left-wing culture that allegedly dominates the ABC.[35] Others, like Labor's communications spokesperson, Senator Stephen Conroy, expressed concern about Mr Scott's Liberal links.[36] Long-time ABC journalist, Quentin Dempster, described him simply as 'competent and professional, and ... acceptable to the Government'.[37] How Scott's career at the ABC turns out remains to be seen, but it is unlikely that the appointment was devoid of political influence.

Of course, the ABC has always been subjected to political interference. Its role in political discourse makes it an obvious target for all governments. *Sydney Morning Herald* columnist Alan Ramsay has suggested that during Labor's thirteen years in office between 1983 and 1996, slightly less than half of appointees to the ABC Board had 'obvious party political connections, while two of them came from among the ranks of its political opponents'.[38] Former Labor opposition communications spokesperson Lindsay Tanner has publicly conceded that a number of appointments made during the Hawke and Keating years were tainted because of the appointees' links to the Labor Party.[39] Yet, while past governments have been guilty of intruding in the affairs of the ABC, the extent to which this has occurred under the Howard

Government is unprecedented. The overwhelming majority of appointees have had a political flavour and some are unabashed ideological warriors. As Inglis has said, there are more party political appointments 'now than there has been at any time between 1983 and 1995'.[40]

The Australian Heritage Council

The stacking of the ABC Board is similar to that which has occurred in the Australian Heritage Commission, now the Australian Heritage Council. The commission's most important task used to be the maintenance of the Register of the National Estate, a list of sites of heritage significance that were partially protected under the *Australian Heritage Commission Act 1975*. Control of the listing process gave the commission considerable power as it had the capacity to influence government development and approval processes and to shape how Australia's history was recorded, recognised and conveyed to the public. However, the commission's influence over both economic and cultural issues meant that it could easily be drawn into conflict with the government of the day. The Howard Government recognised this and has gone about 'reforming' both the structure of the commission and its membership.

The major restructuring of the commission occurred in January 2004 when it was abolished and replaced by the council. Unlike the commission, the council is not a statutory authority, but rather an advisory body prescribed under legislation. This change is important as it has restricted the council's capacity to undertake activities independently of the government.[41] Even more significant were the alterations made in relation to the Commonwealth's heritage lists and the council's control over them.

The council has retained control of the Register of the National Estate, but places on the register no longer receive any additional statutory protection. That is, it has control of a list that serves only as an educational device rather than a means of assisting in the protection of the listed sites. In addition, the government has created a National Heritage List, which is supposed to contain places that are of national (as opposed to state, regional or local) heritage significance. In effect, the National Heritage List has now replaced the register as the nation's pre-eminent list of heritage sites.[42] Consistent with the government's philosophy on public agencies, the power to include places on the National Heritage List was given to the environment minister rather than the council. The council's only involvement in the listing processes is in an advisory capacity. It is responsible for evaluating whether nominated sites meet the listing criteria, but the minister decides whether a place is included on the list and can refuse to list a site even if the council decides that it is of national heritage significance.

These changes have removed the independence from the listing process and have left the National Heritage List vulnerable to being used for political purposes—and the government has wasted little time in exploiting this vulnerability. Reflecting the Coalition's ideological preferences, the National Heritage List is currently weighted heavily in favour of colonial heritage and post-1788 sites. Places of natural and Indigenous heritage significance have been largely ignored.[43] The government has also been careful to ensure that the places that have been listed are unlikely to be threatened by current or future developments.

In addition, the government has carefully timed listing announcements (often in violation of statutory requirements) to either maximise or minimise publicity, depending on what was politically expedient. For example, Treasurer Peter Costello announced the listing of the Melbourne Cricket Ground on the opening day of the Boxing Day test in 2005. Several months later, the government announced the listing of the Australian War Memorial on ANZAC Day. In contrast, Environment Minister Senator Ian Campbell has delayed both rejecting places and announcing rejections, in several instances in breach of his statutory duties, in what appears to have been an attempt to avoid negative publicity.[44] Senator Campbell has been quite brazen about his use of these tactics and the disregard of statutory time frames. In response to questioning from Labor Senator Kim Carr in May 2006 about why he had failed to comply with the legal requirements, he simply said that, 'I make announcements of my decisions at a time when it maximises the benefit of building the public awareness of Australia's heritage'.[45]

Along with the reform of the heritage regime, the government has also made a number of politically tainted appointments to both the commission and the council. In 1998, the then minister for the Environment and Heritage, Senator Robert Hill, appointed long-time Liberal supporter and former mayor of Woollahra Municipal Council Peter King as the chair of the commission. Mr King had no obvious qualifications for the job as he was a Sydney barrister who specialised in admiralty, international trade and constitutional law. However, his political affiliations were solid, a fact vividly demonstrated when he was found to be actively campaigning for the Liberals in the federal seat of Wentworth in Sydney while still the chair of the commission. In an interview with the ABC in July 2001, he stated bluntly that he was 'certainly working very, very hard to ensure that the continued Liberal representation in Wentworth is maintained'.[46] Mr King subsequently became the federal Liberal member for Wentworth in the 2001 election.

His replacement was Tom Harley, great-grandson of Australia's second prime minister, Alfred Deakin. Much like Mr King, Harley has no formal training or expertise in the evaluation of heritage sites, but he does have extensive links with the Liberal Party. In addition to being friends with a number of people in the government, he is chairman of the Liberal think tank, the Menzies Research Centre. He is also an executive at BHP Billiton, a position that has given rise to several conflicts of interest as he has been required to evaluate listing nominations that could affect the financial interests of the company.[47] When the commission was dissolved in 2004 Mr Harley became the chair of the new council.

The Fair Pay Commission

The Howard Government has made substantial changes to Australia's industrial relations system. One of the most significant modifications has been to diminish the role of the Australian Industrial Relations Commission (AIRC). Prior to 1996, the AIRC had broad powers to settle disputes and set minimum wages and conditions. Soon after coming to power the Howard Government passed the *Workplace Relations Act 1996*, which restricted the ability of the AIRC to settle disputes and limited its ability to set award conditions. These amendments affected the ability of the AIRC to perform its functions, yet the evidence suggests it quickly adapted to the changes such that it remained an important player in the industrial relations system.[48]

The Workchoices legislation that was passed in 2005 has scaled back the powers of the AIRC even further. It is no longer involved in setting minimum wages and conditions. These powers have been transferred to the newly established Fair Pay Commission, while the AIRC's ability to settle disputes has also been eroded. Further, several appointments have been made to the AIRC that have raised questions about its independence, including Jonathan Hamberger's appointment as a Senior Deputy President in 2003.[49] Hamberger previously worked as an adviser to Peter Reith, the Workplace Relations minister (1997–2001) who presided over the waterfront dispute in 1998. After leaving Reith's office, he was appointed deputy and then head of the Commonwealth Office of the Employment Advocate, which is responsible for vetting and registering Australian Workplace Agreements (AWAs). While serving as the employment advocate, Hamberger publicly criticised the Labor Party's policy in 2001 to abolish AWAs, a move that the *Australian Financial Review* described as 'an unusual public intervention by a senior government official into a political debate'.[50] Hamberger claimed scrapping AWAs would create 'a real problem' for business and suggested that the shift from AWAs to common law contracts would leave workers worse off.[51] After his time at the Office of the Employment Advocate, he was appointed to the AIRC.[52]

Not surprisingly, the first Fair Pay Commission is awash with conservatives. *Sydney Morning Herald* columnist Adele Horin summed it up when she wrote:

> John Howard has discarded even the pretence of balance in his choice of members for the Fair Pay Commission . . . The fate of at least 20 per cent of the workforce will be in the hands of five social and economic conservatives, who will make pay decisions for those at the bottom.[53]

The commissioners include former ABC Board member and conservative labour market economist Judith Sloan, who is a member of the Centre for Independent Studies' council of academic advisers and has been involved in a number of events organised by the H.R. Nicholls Society, a right-wing organisation devoted to the promotion of an unregulated labour market and the destruction of trade unions. At one H.R. Nicholls function she reportedly asked the audience, rhetorically, the difference between the ACTU and Jurassic Park, to which she answered, 'one is a group of dinosaurs hanging around waiting to get extinct . . . the other is a film'.[54]

The influence of the right-wing Centre for Independent Studies on the Fair Pay Commission does not stop at Judith Sloan. The current chair of the commission is Professor Ian Harper, who is also a member of the centre's council of academic advisers. Several of Harper's articles have been published by the centre, including one in which he condemns debt forgiveness for third world countries and suggests that 'Christians need to approach the issue with a soft heart and hard head'.[55] Harper is known for his skills as an economist, but his strong religious faith, involvement in a company that went broke after allegedly trading while insolvent and opposition to the concept of a 'fair and reasonable wage'[56] have led to questions being raised about his independence.[57]

Two other notable appointees on the Fair Pay Commission are Patrick McClure, former head of Mission Australia, and Michael O'Hagan, who owns the removal company MiniMovers. Mission Australia was awarded millions of dollars of Job Network contracts by the federal government while Mr McClure headed the organisation and he is known to have 'long-time links to the Liberal Party'.[58] While it is not known whether O'Hagan is intimately associated with the Coalition, he has been a strong supporter of the deregulation of the labour market and AWAs. The MiniMovers' website boasts that,

> ... [i]n 2004, the Prime Minister, Mr John Howard called in 'for coffee' at our Rocklea depot because of our ongoing policy to staffing and conditions. The introduction of AWAs (Australian Workplace Agreements) in 2003, allowed MiniMovers to offer a more flexible workplace, unlimited career opportunities and a lot more ongoing benefits for our staff.[59]

O'Hagan's enthusiasm for AWAs was so great that the government made him an 'Australian Workplace Agreement ambassador'.[60] After becoming an ambassador O'Hagan attended a number of government business functions, where he extolled the virtues of AWAs.[61] He has also featured prominently in numerous government publications on AWAs[62] and in several articles published in Murdoch newspapers supporting the rise of AWAs and criticising Labor's plans to abolish them.[63] Workplace Relations Minister Kevin Andrews even attended a MiniMovers function to present one of its workers with the 500 000th AWA to have been signed since their introduction.[64]

Although the government has been clinical in the execution of its plans to limit the independence of the public agencies that regulate the workplace, it recognises that it is important for these agencies to be seen to be independent. To date, most of the concern about the independence and workplace change has focused on the Office of Workplace Services (OWS). In March 2006 the minister, Kevin Andrews, announced that the OWS had been made an 'independent agency with an expanded scope to monitor workplaces and give advice to employees and employers under the WorkChoices reforms'.[65] Yet, the OWS was only made an executive agency under the Public Service Act, meaning its director can be hired and fired at the whim of the minister, and it has limited powers to act independently of the government. Not surprisingly, since the minister's announcement, OWS documents have been leaked to the media on several occasions in ways that have assisted the government.[66]

National Museum of Australia

The purpose of the National Museum of Australia is to develop and maintain a collection of historical material and to exhibit material that relates to Australia's past, present and future.[67] Like the ABC and the Australian Heritage Council, the National Museum requires independence from the government to perform these functions effectively. Excessive political involvement would compromise the duty of the museum to present materials in a way that accurately reflects Australia's history and society.

When the museum's premises first opened in 2001 it was unclear whether the Howard Government would give the museum room to operate independently. On the one hand, it appointed Dawn Casey, a well-regarded public servant and winner of several public service medals, as director of the museum. Counteracting this, it placed a number of well-known conservative ideologues on the council of the museum, including News Ltd columnist and former Howard speechwriter Christopher Pearson (who was also appointed to the SBS Board),[68] former Liberal Party president and Fraser Government minister Tony Staley, and David Barnett, who is a conservative writer, former press secretary of Malcolm Fraser and authorised biographer of John Howard. Barnett is also married to Pru Goward, the federal Sex Discrimination Commissioner from 2001 and endorsed Liberal candidate for the 2007 New South Wales state election.

Initially, the museum appeared to function reasonably effectively. In its first eighteen months it attracted over 1.3 million visitors, and the 2001/02 annual report of the museum was gushing in its praise of the work done by Casey and her colleagues, with the chairman of the council stating that 'all members of Council join me in congratulating the Director, Dawn Casey, and her staff on the Museum's outstanding success'.[69] Yet it was apparent even before the museum opened that there was disquiet in the council about the exhibits and the museum's portrayal of Australian history, particularly early colonial history and the frontier conflicts between Aborigines and European settlers.

Grievances about the exhibits in the museum were first expressed by Barnett. In late 2000, Barnett wrote a memo where he described the exhibit on the stolen generation as a 'victim episode'[70] and complained about the 'reworking of Australian history into political correctness'.[71] His objections were supported by fellow council member Christopher Pearson, as well as by conservative historian Keith Windschuttle, who argued in an article published in the magazine *Quadrant* in September 2001 that 'you have to run a gauntlet of cultural propaganda' in the Indigenous galleries, describing the accounts of frontier relations as 'fictitious', and concluding by stating that the 'National Museum is a profound intellectual mistake as well as a great waste of public money'.[72] Other conservative media columnists like Miranda Devine, News Ltd columnist Piers Ackerman and Angela Shanahan, who writes for *The Australian*, also championed the conservative cause. Devine even described the underlying message of the museum as 'one of sneering ridicule for white Australia', and said the 'whole museum is a lie'.[73] It appeared that the conservatives did not approve of the museum's pluralistic style that attempted to find a place for different perspectives on history. They wanted an approach that was more celebratory of colonial history and the achievements of western culture, and that dwelt less on the negatives associated with European settlement.[74]

Upon receiving Barnett's criticisms, Chairman Tony Staley referred them to historian Graeme Davison and asked him to assess their validity. His response was categorical. In an article published in *The Age* in December 2002, Davison stated that, 'after carefully reviewing them, I found that almost none of his criticisms could be supported by reputable scholarship'.[75] However, this did not satisfy the conservatives. According to some accounts, the board became 'paralysed by trench warfare waged mainly by the revisionists',[76] who saw the museum as a major theatre for the culture wars.[77]

In late 2002, Arts Minister Senator Rod Kemp decided to renew Dawn Casey's contract as director for only a year rather than three to five years as had been expected. Not long after, Staley announced a review of the museum that was to be headed by John Carroll, a social conservative who at the time was a reader in sociology at La Trobe University. The other panel members were Richard Longes (a director of several companies including Investec Australia Ltd), Patricia Vickers-Rich (a professor of palaeontology) and Philip Jones (the curator of the South Australian Museum who played a crucial role in the Hindmarsh Island affair as a critic of the 'secret women's business'; he is also a good friend of Christopher Pearson).[78] Interestingly, none of the panel members were historians. When the review was subsequently released in July 2003, while it did not support the claims of systematic bias, it found there were pockets of bias, it was critical of the depiction of some of the negative effects of European settlement and it called for greater attention to be given to a grand narrative and the main themes of Australian history like discovery, exploration and sporting and business achievements.[79]

When Dawn Casey departed from the museum in December 2003 she was followed by her supporters on the council, Marcus Besen, Sharon Brown and Ron Webb. Their terms on the council were not renewed by Senator Kemp, and in their place came several conservative appointments including religious broadcaster John Fleming and historian John Hirst (who is now deputy chair). Casey was subsequently replaced by Craddock Morton, who had previously worked in the corporate and business division of the Department of Communications, Information Technology and the Arts.

Conclusion

The campaign devised by John Howard and his close confidants in 1995 and 1996 to infiltrate and restructure public agencies to limit their independence has been executed with precision and to excellent effect. Over the past decade, federal public agencies have been systematically stacked with individuals who have close ties to the Coalition or the conservative cause. Pamela Williams, writing in the *Australian Financial Review*, described it accurately:

> . . . the men and women appointed to positions of power and
> influence across the country form a conservative river as deep

as it is wide. It flows through the bureaucracy, government bodies and regulators, tribunals for refugees and industrial relations, cushy diplomatic posts, Telstra, the ABC, and arts bodies and cultural institutions. It runs from friends and mates to career bureaucrats, from lowly quangos to the gilded echelons of the High Court. It is the fountainhead of Liberal influence for years to come.[80]

At the same time as boards have been stacked, the government has gone about restructuring public agencies with the objective of limiting their independence and placing as many as possible under the direct control of ministers. Some of the restructuring could be defensible on the grounds of financial accountability. However, the blanket manner in which the ministerial-centralisation approach has been applied demonstrates that the enhancement of control and limitation of independent and dissenting opinion have been the main drivers behind the reforms.

Apart from the more high-profile instances discussed above, there is a plethora of examples that could be used to demonstrate how the government has gone about undermining the independence of public agencies. For example, the appointment of prohibition advocate Major Brian Watters of the Salvation Army to head the Australian National Council on Drugs was controversial, as was his replacement, Dr John Herron, a former Liberal Senator for Queensland and minister for Aboriginal and Torres Strait Islander Affairs (1996–2001). Of similar interest was the placement of Robert Gerard, a long-standing member of, and donor to, the Liberal Party, on the board of the Reserve Bank of Australia, the appointment of former National Party leader Tim Fischer to chair Tourism Australia, and Bruce Lloyd's (former deputy leader of the National Party) chairmanship of the Australian Landcare Council and membership of the Natural Heritage Trust Advisory Committee.

The Labor Party has denied that it has a hit list like that prepared by John Howard in the lead-up to the 1996 election, yet Senator John Faulkner's office has drafted a document that outlines a large number of politically tainted appointments to departments, public agencies and other governmental posts. Given the extent of the stacking, there is no doubt that when the Labor Party regains office it will feel compelled to rid public agencies of many of the conservative appointees. It may also undo some of the restructuring that has occurred, although there will no doubt be a temptation to constrain the independence of agencies to keep them under the control of ministers. It is to be hoped, however, that Labor will resist replacing political appointees with others of a different stripe and that it will take measures to re-establish the independence of public agencies, including those discussed here.

The cyclical nature of the changes to the structure of, and personnel in, public agencies that is a product of political meddling undermines public confidence in these institutions and affects the performance of their intended functions. To protect these organisations from a destructive, politically driven process, changes must be made to how appointments are made. The obvious starting point would be to establish an independent body that is responsible for regulating appointments, as has occurred in the United Kingdom. People of all political persuasions have a role to play in public agencies, but problems arise when representation is weighted too heavily in favour of the political interests of the government of the day. An independent appointment commission could lower the risk of this occurring and help ensure that a diverse range of interests are represented in agencies that serve the public interest.

All political parties need to decide whether the concentration of power is in the long-term interests of Australia's democracy. In an era when the foundations of responsible government are in decline, there is a strong argument for the dispersal of power to independent public agencies and for greater reliance to be placed on avenues of accountability that are not overly dependent on ministers and Cabinet.

9

The military and intelligence services

Andrew Wilkie

Australia's military and intelligence services are essential for the defence of the country and the fulfilment of our international security and humanitarian obligations. Everything about the services—legislation, oversight, operations, culture, structure, resources and processes—should be directed at ensuring they operate effectively to that end. They should be environments of excellence involving some of the best thinkers and managers in the country.

The military and intelligence services should be no different to the rest of the Australian Public Service (APS), where 'principles of apoliticism, impartiality, professionalism, responsiveness and accountability ... [should be] ... at the heart of strong, productive relationships between the APS and the elected government'.[1] Governments should respond by respecting the independence of the services and by always being careful to not cross the line between governance and politics. They should only interact with the military and intelligence services as much as is needed to oversee the proper operation of the services in accordance with legislation and the pursuit of strictly non-political outcomes.

But the way the military and intelligence services *should* be is a long way from how things really are, because the Howard Government has made, and continues to make, serious and specific efforts to politicise its relationship with the services, manipulate their conduct and misuse their efforts. The situation has deteriorated to the point where there is now little scope in the military and intelligence services for the high-level expression of views contrary to those of the Howard Government. The norm has become routine border security and counter-terrorism operations, and risky and seemingly endless deployments to far-flung Afghanistan and Iraq, and consequently the capacity of the services to deal with the most pressing threats to Australian security has been jeopardised.

Manipulation of security advice

The Coalition Government has shaped the military and intelligence services by vetting senior appointments and by installing trusted players in key positions. For instance, the head of the Office of National Assessments (ONA), Peter Varghese, appointed in 2004, and the head of the Australian Security Intelligence Organisation (ASIO), Paul O'Sullivan, appointed in 2005, are both former members of John Howard's inner circle of advisers.[2] Moreover, Defence Intelligence Organisation (DIO) Head Maurie McNarn, appointed in 2005, is regarded by many military officers as someone unlikely to cause the government any angst.[3] Others can judge the competence and ethics of these men, but at the very least such appointments should raise questions in people's minds about the independence of the services at a time when the public needs to have confidence that all is well.

The Coalition Government's appointments are certainly not causing too many problems for it these days. For instance, there has been no concern expressed by O'Sullivan about the government's strengthening of national counter-terrorism legislation despite his predecessor, Dennis Richardson, telling a parliamentary committee that ASIO did not need additional powers.[4] And there was the curious scene, in Senate Budget estimates, where Varghese aligned with the government's evasions over the Australian Wheat Board (AWB) bribery scandal by refusing to answer questions on the matter.[5]

Aiding the government's efforts to shape the military and intelligence services is the power invested in the heads of agencies to grant and rescind the security clearances needed for such work. The aim of the security clearance process is to filter out questionable and unreliable job applicants and serving officials. But it has been tightened up significantly over recent years as the security agencies have responded to direct pressure from the government to prevent any more embarrassing leaks or troublesome outspoken officials.[6] So whereas the services had been trying for some years to better incorporate the intellectual diversity of the Australian community, now they have been pressured to lurch back towards the days of only recruiting the most politically reliable people.

Reinforcing the Howard Government's pressure on the staff of the military and intelligence services is the imbalance in legislation, which offers virtually no protection to officials troubled by government misconduct and in fact threatens harsh punishment if they speak out about their concerns. Significantly, there is still no Commonwealth whistleblower legislation that would protect a security official who discloses information specifically about government misconduct. The closest is the *Public Service Act 1999*[7] and the *Ombudsman Act 1976*,[8] but these are only relevant to public servants reporting breaches of the APS Code of Conduct, or for outspoken officials hoping to avoid civil proceedings. By contrast, a swag of legislation gives unambiguous power to the heads of public service agencies to hire and fire, and therefore to potentially help governments take retribution against officials revealing official misconduct. Significantly, the *Crimes Act 1914*[9] specifies two years imprisonment for any official disclosing virtually any material they obtain from their workplace. The *Criminal Code Act 1995*[10] specifies 25 years jail when disclosure of information is intended to harm national security, as the government may argue is the case when officials speak out during times of conflict. Very tough penalties also exist for anyone publicising material provided by an official, making the job of a would-be security whistleblower or leaker of sensitive information all the more difficult.[11]

To the degree that such legislation predates the Coalition's election, the government's mischief is in the way it has created a climate in which officials have become more concerned that existing penalties could be used against them. Reinforcing this, however, has been the government's interest in strengthening the legislation, such as the 2002 amendments to the *Criminal Code Act 1995* that increase the penalty from seven to 25 years for any disclosure 'intended' to harm security.[12]

The cards are further stacked against officials concerned with government misconduct by the government's enthusiasm for calling in the police to investigate leaks, often at enormous cost. Between 2000 and 2004, for example, the Australian Federal Police (AFP) spent about 33 000 staff hours investigating some 64 leaks from government agencies at a cost of almost $200 000 plus wages.[13] A conservative calculation would translate that into a total cost to taxpayers of $2 million or so. Another 47 inquiries kept the AFP busy in the three years before that.[14]

A softening of the oversight regime has further enabled the politicisation of the military and intelligence services in recent years. For a start, the federal parliament's role in national security matters has been reduced almost to irrelevance by the Howard Government's practice of dealing with security issues elsewhere, in particular within the Prime Minister's own department and in the National Security Committee of Cabinet. Not even the decision to commit the country to war in Iraq was decided upon in the parliament. This aversion to proper process has spilled over into the committee system—in particular to estimates hearings—where the government habitually manipulates the attendance of officials and the scope of responses that those attending might give (see Chapter 10 for more detail). Still memorable is the way in which key witnesses were prevented from involvement in the Select Committee on a Certain Maritime Incident investigating the so-called 'children overboard' affair, including the key witness, Mike Scrafton, who was muzzled until after he left the public service some years later.[15] The government's interest in winding back the role of Senate committees even further, including by reducing their number and ensuring they are always chaired by a government member, was signalled by Finance Minister Senator Nick Minchin in June 2006.[16]

Compounding the problem is the Labor Party's aversion to politicising security issues.[17]

Ministerial oversight has also deteriorated significantly in recent years. Ministers now excuse military and intelligence failures. An illustration of this, in 2004, was Howard's unqualified praise for the head of ONA, Kim Jones, during the heated public discussion about the absence of weapons of mass destruction (WMD) in post-invasion Iraq,[18] and Defence Minister Robert Hill's similar public praise for the head of DIO, Frank Lewincamp, at about the same time.[19] According to the Howard Government, the heads of the two crucial intelligence assessment agencies did a good job on Iraq, even though their apparent misreading of the situation constituted a remarkable intelligence failure. Lewincamp was even awarded the Public Service Medal.[20] Such behaviour was repeated when disgraced Immigration head, Bill Farmer, was awarded an Order of Australia[21] and given the plum ambassador's job in Jakarta in 2005, not long before the release of the report about the wrongful immigration detention of Australian citizen Cornelia Rau.[22] This type of unqualified praise was repeated in 2006, when the government refused to acknowledge any bureaucratic failure regarding Australian company AWB's payment of bribes to Iraq during Saddam Hussein's rule,[23] and again when they initially failed to acknowledge any Army ineptitude over the repatriation of the wrong body and conflicting public explanations following the death of Australian soldier Jake Kovco in Iraq.[24] All of this fosters the loyalty of senior public servants as they become increasingly indebted to the government and absorbed into its pattern of misconduct.

Government control of the terms of reference for ad hoc official inquiries compromises the apparently apolitical accountability of such mechanisms. There are numerous examples of the problem, so many in fact that one might suspect a pattern of deliberate obfuscation and deception about the relationship between the government and the military and intelligence services. For instance, the Parliamentary Joint Committee on ASIO, ASIS (Australian Secret Intelligence Service) and DSD (Defence Signals Directorate) inquiry into the Iraq war was not empowered to look beyond the missing WMD to the broader government case for war.[25] Nor was the subsequent inquiry into the war—ordered by the Prime Minister, who personally directed inquisitor Philip Flood—empowered to look at the government's relationship with the services.[26] And Terence Cole's inquiry into AWB was also not permitted to look specifically at the government's involvement in that issue.[27]

Such overt politicisation now apparently extends deep into the military and intelligence services. The terms of reference for the Defence inquiry into the Jake Kovco debacle were reported to have excluded a requirement to consider the involvement of Defence Minister Brendan Nelson, even though the string of inaccurate public utterances by Nelson was central to the matter.[28]

Misuse of security resources

The politicisation of the military and intelligence services is compounded by the Howard Government's routine use of the services to pursue political goals well beyond Australia's genuine national security objectives. Of course, the degree to which a military or intelligence operation is driven by politics, rather than by genuine security considerations, is often difficult to gauge accurately or absolutely. For instance, while the run of counter-terrorism exercises and occasional well-publicised raids in recent years have merely had a strong whiff of politics about them, other military and intelligence operations have appeared less ambiguously to be political theatre.

The extraordinary effort that has gone into border security since about 1999 has been a primarily political exercise. For instance, the use of DSD to eavesdrop on the *Tampa* crew's communications—including to Australia—and the show put on by the Special Air Service when they 'stormed' the vessel were designed to make the government look tough on border security before the 2001 federal election. They were, however, a gross misuse of military and intelligence resources. Even the continued involvement of Australian troops in Iraq is much more political than practical; because the operation is so tiny and has been mostly out of harm's way—Al Muthanna Province, where Australian forces focused initially, is a relatively peaceful area—it can be considered little more than a political gesture in support of the US Bush Administration. This would appear to also be the view of the American frontline commanders in Iraq, who have reportedly been dismayed that their Australian colleagues have not been allowed by the Australian Government to do anything more effective.[29] Whether government announcements about taking on a more risky role in Iraq signal a real departure from this situation remains to be seen.

Much has been written in recent years about the way in which the Howard Government has sought to exploit the so-called politics of fear. In other words, the exploitation of people's xenophobia for political benefit, for instance, by fostering fear about refugees and Muslims.[30] The effect on the security agencies of such politics has been to distract them as they struggle to cope with the demands of both the blatant politicisation of their work (such as hunting asylum-seeker boats) and the knock-on demands for even better security by an increasingly fearful public. Illustrating the way in which the government sometimes loses control of its cultivation of xenophobia are the regular public demands for better security at regional Australian airports—an impossibly expensive challenge sometimes in marginal electorates.

The risks of politicisation

The politicisation of the military and intelligence services has degraded them and weakened Australia's capacity to safeguard national security. This would be alarming at any time, but even more so now in light of the significant security challenges confronting Australia. These include, in particular, challenges such as the proliferation of nuclear weapons and climate change, as well as the lesser, but still complex, unconventional threats of terrorism, people-smuggling, illicit drugs, and so on. Climate change in particular will require a sophisticated response by Australian military and intelligence services as rising sea levels, shortages of fresh water and food, and extreme weather events cause unprecedented intra-state hardship and inter-state unrest in Australia's area of strategic interest.[31] Australia will only be able to deal with such challenges if it possesses the very best security policies and resources. But the limited terrorist threat highlighted by the 11 September 2001 attacks in the United States, and the long-running stand-off with Saddam Hussein in Iraq were in fact straightforward security challenges. Still, the Howard

Government was incapable of responding to them sensibly and ethically.

Fortunately, for much of the time political appointments in the military and intelligence services are of little consequence in day-to-day operations. The services just get on with their work and generally make a pretty good job of it, even when the most obsequious senior managers are at the helm. However, problems do occur whenever a controversial national security issue arises, at which time the need for unbiased support is critical. The failure of the military and intelligence services to challenge the government over its enthusiasm to join in the Iraq war is a standout example of the perils that can be visited upon Australia when politicisation skews advice and buries differences of opinion. Although both official Australian inquiries into the war made findings indicating government misconduct,[32] the services never once challenged the government over its consistent exaggerations about the threat posed by Saddam Hussein and the urgent need to deal with it. Challenging, in this instance, did not necessitate causing embarrassment for the government; a discreet meeting was all that was required to push the point home that the official case for war was significantly at odds with the information held by the services. There is no evidence that any such meeting was ever held. Nor was there any shortage of opportunities to raise the matter, because ONA fact-checked all of the Prime Minister's main speeches on Iraq,[33] and at any time could have pointed out the gap between the weight of evidence and the thrust of the speeches. It never did. The military and intelligence services' buckling over Iraq contributed indirectly to the needless deaths of tens of thousands of Iraqis and the suffering of countless more.

And it doesn't stop there. For instance, the reluctance of ONA and DIO to push hard against the Howard Government's prevarication during the pre-independence violence in East Timor in 1999 helped to delay foreign intervention while countless people were being killed. So too, ONA's disinclination to tell the government how bad the situation was in Afghanistan in 2002 supported the dangerous return from Australia of Afghan asylum seekers. An intelligence assessment I prepared detailing the awful situation in Afghanistan was adjusted and delayed by ONA because it contradicted the government's public assertion about the much-improved situation there and policy to return asylum seekers. In both examples, Australian intelligence agencies put political interest and self-interest ahead of public interest because the agencies believed they could not risk their own 'relevance' in case the government decided to turn elsewhere for its needs.

Exit, voice and loyalty

All the laws, checks, pressures and oversight failures in the military and intelligence services build a comprehensive deterrent to dissent. But they are still only a deterrent. Officials retain the right and capacity to resist and speak out. At the end of the day, it is their decision and their decision only. All are potential dissenters.

So why don't more break ranks when security issues are contentious and government conduct is found wanting? Why, for instance, didn't many officials speak out when the Prime Minister and Defence Minister Peter Reith claimed repeatedly— and misleadingly—that asylum seekers had thrown their children overboard in 2001? Part of the explanation is broadly consistent with the thesis articulated by American academic Albert Hirschman in *Exit, Voice, and Loyalty* almost 40 years ago.[34] He described how some disaffected workers will leave their organisation in the belief that they are important enough, or acting with others in such numbers, that their act of exit or subsequent absence from the workplace might bring about positive change. Many disaffected workers would, however, be unlikely to choose this option, thinking instead that they are so influential that they have the power in their voice to bring about change from within. Moreover, some of those deciding not to exit would instead hope to deploy more creative ways of bringing about internal change, despite the inherent difficulty of this approach in many large organisations. Over the top of this Hirschman lays loyalty, which can stifle exit and promote voice, including among uninfluential workers, so long as they believe that someone else will speak up or that somehow things will get better. 'As a rule, then', Hirschman explains, 'loyalty holds exit at bay and activates voice'.[35]

Loyalty is certainly relevant to understanding the apparently low level of dissent in the military and intelligence services. Officials feel morally and legally bound to follow orders, regardless of their view of the merit of those orders, and many regard transgressors as traitors. Many of those in the military and intelligence services also have an elevated and distorted sense of what they regard as loyalty to country. This of course is nothing new, as there has long been an attraction to public service among those with a strong sense of patriotism. The Howard Government's efforts to play up nationalism might be expected to have fuelled this phenomenon, and it probably has in the intelligence agencies, although enduring recruiting difficulties suggest other factors at work with the military when it comes to young flag-wrapped nationalists actually risking being shot at.

The paucity of dissenters in the military and intelligence services is, in addition, a product of the nature of public service, or in fact any organisation. For instance, some officials will always share the government's view on an issue, right or wrong. Others will be prepared to go along with virtually anything, so long as it advances their careers. Many will probably give a government the benefit of the doubt unless they are closely associated with a controversial issue. And almost all will be financial conscripts, especially in a small city like Canberra. On balance, leaving the public service in controversial circumstances can carry too great an exit price for many officials to seriously contemplate, even more so when thrown into the mix are the difficulties of hanging on to friends, finding work afterwards and simply staying alive— unlike British Iraq war whistleblower David Kelly, who took his own life in 2003.[36]

Faced with such a list of consequences it is no surprise that military and intelligence officials often look for easier or more innovative ways to right the wrongs they detect. Some will consider leaking sensitive information to outsiders in the hope of having the issue highlighted. Others will continue to try and bring about change from within, limiting the expression of their concerns in order to stay out of trouble, but hoping to have some chance of influencing superiors and politicians. If they are senior enough they might achieve some success this way. But such an approach can be the resort of those prone to overestimating their importance to the government or to those who seek, consciously or subconsciously, an excuse for inaction.

Some case studies

Some military and intelligence officials manage to rise above all this. For instance, in 2004 Defence intelligence officer Lance Collins wrote to the Prime Minister personally 'about the failure of institutional controls over the Australian intelligence system', and went on to speak about his concerns on television and in a book.[37] Also in 2004 Mike Scrafton broke his silence on the 'children overboard' affair when he wrote to *The Australian*[38] newspaper to reveal that on 7 November 2001—the day before Howard told the press club that asylum seekers had thrown their children into the water and two days before the 2001 federal election—he spoke to Howard three times and told him that '. . . no one in Defence that I had dealt with on the matter still believed any children were thrown overboard'.[39] More recently, former senior United Nations weapons inspector Rod Barton went to the media and then wrote a book to reveal how information on Iraqi WMD had been manipulated, and how Iraqi prisoners were mistreated.[40] All served the public interest significantly by eventually speaking up about the controversial matters that preoccupied them.

But such people have invariably been assailed by a government keen to put troublemakers in their place and to send a strong message to other officials not to step out of line. For instance, Collins's call for a Royal Commission was dismissed by Howard[41] and he was eventually forced out of Defence by the 'blowtorching process'.[42] Scrafton's evidence was criticised by the government as 'implausible, irrational and evasive', and the timing of his claims as 'politically strategic'.[43] Barton was reportedly marginalised at the insistence of Howard's staff,[44] and even ridiculed by Howard himself who pushed the view that 'it's quite common for people with no understanding of the process, or little understanding of the process, to misunderstand the things they see . . .'.[45] Moreover, Collins, Scrafton and Barton were eventually passed over by national media generally disinclined to run too long with any one story, especially those dealing with complicated security issues. So even though this handful of important witnesses all came across as credible and were vindicated in their concerns, they probably still appeared to many members of the public as exceptions rather than reflective of broader anxiety about government misconduct within the military and intelligence services. Unfortunately, however, the government misconduct signalled by Collins, Scrafton and Barton is widespread; so much so, and in so many forms, that the pattern formed is just as worrying as the individual examples.

Take, for instance, Kate Burton.[46] She joined ONA in 2001 as a strategic analyst and went on to work on transnational issues. But soon after joining ONA she became alert to the politicised culture in the security agencies and in particular to ONA's obsession with 'customer focus'—in other words, of delivering what the Howard Government wanted, rather than needed. Burton became disenchanted with ONA's pro-US bias and also refused to work on the People Smuggling Task Force because of her revulsion at the government's policy. In 2003, barely halfway through her contract, she left ONA and went on, in 2005, to secure a position on the staff of the Parliamentary Joint Committee on ASIO, ASIS and DSD. But by then the government was alert to her 'disloyalty', and she was summoned by her new manager on the first day to be told that some members of the committee were concerned that her perceived political views could lead to a conflict of interest with the committee's needs. Burton accepted the offer of a move onto the staff of another committee.

Another interesting case is that of former ONA officer Anthony Billingsley. He had served for many years in the Middle East with the Department of Foreign Affairs and Trade, and was a senior Middle East analyst in ONA during 2002 and 2003. But Billingsley, despite being well placed to offer an informed opinion on the problems with the official case for war, did not appear as a witness at the inquiry into the Iraq war conducted by the Parliamentary Joint Committee on ASIO, ASIS and DSD in 2003.[47] This was not because he was suspected of wanting to deliberately cause problems for the government, but because he was likely to embarrass it nonetheless by simply revealing what he knew. Nor did ONA grant him permission later in 2003, shortly after his resignation from ONA, to speak about the war at a lecture organised by the Macquarie University Centre for Middle East and North African studies.[48] This was an extraordinary intercession by ONA, not only because its officers had previously been free to write and speak about their area of expertise after leaving (so long as sensitive information was never disclosed), but also because this specific commitment had been approved by ONA earlier in the year.

Nor was Billingsley's experience a one-off, for none of the Middle East analysts, or even the crucial senior strategic analyst covering the bulk of the Iraq workload, appeared before the Parliamentary Joint Committee's inquiry. The involvement of the senior strategic issues analyst in particular—responsible for most of the assessments on Iraq—would have allowed him to explain the significant shift he and his superiors brought to the more measured assessments drafted by his predecessor, Carl Ungerer, who covered Iraq from 1999 until 2002. More than a dozen reports were written on Iraq during this period, including several joint reports with DIO. At no stage did Ungerer argue that the evidence on Iraq's WMD programs was conclusive. However, the senior management of ONA consistently sought to underplay ambiguities about the Iraqi WMD threat because to do otherwise would have been inconsistent with their, and the Howard Government's, more hawkish position. So time and again Ungerer drafted relatively measured assessments that portrayed Saddam Hussein's potential WMD capability as limited and unsophisticated, only to see his analysis 'hardened' as it went up the line.[49]

Clinton Fernandes provides yet another telling example of the treatment meted out to those who maintain their independence of thought in the military and intelligence services.[50] Fernandes was forced to fight a protracted battle with Defence—which he eventually won—before he could publish his Army-approved PhD thesis about Australia's involvement in East Timor. His book, *Reluctant Saviour*,[51] was prepared using unclassified material but was critical of the Howard Government, and national security and secrecy laws were invoked in the attempt to stop it.

My own experience is also relevant. I resigned from ONA in March 2003 over the government's deceitful case for the invasion of Iraq. That I felt the need to blow the whistle points to the role for dissent over government misconduct, regardless of how well the military and intelligence services are working. ONA responded by announcing I was not involved in work on Iraq. The next day a member of Howard's staff advised the media I was mentally unstable, a development discussed with me in detail by the Prime Minister's chief of staff, Arthur Sinodinos, who rang me to claim that Howard had no hand in it. And later that year an official submission was sent to a British inquiry into the war, at which I was appearing, again distancing my work from the Iraq issue. In mid-2003, a secret report I had written on Iraq was leaked to *Herald-Sun* columnist Andrew Bolt in another attempt to discredit me.[52] Although I soon learned that ONA records pointed to a member of Foreign Minister Alexander Downer's staff as being responsible, the leak went uninvestigated for months and has never been resolved. AFP sources have since told me they are pretty sure who leaked the document but are unable to prove it. Moreover, no investigation was ever undertaken, despite the deliberate publication of secret information being a serious criminal offence.

To live with the knowledge that the government is prepared to commit serious crimes to get at you is unpleasant. In some respects, it seems that it is no better than the terrible foreign regimes that it is so quick to criticise. In mid-2004 the government also censored the book I wrote about my resignation, *Axis of Deceit*.[53] This was another intimidating exercise, during which a small number of text deletions were insisted upon, apparently for no reason other than to bully me, my publisher, a documentary-maker with whom I was cooperating at the time and my former colleagues. The whole episode did have a theatrical air about it though: page 155 of the published version contains a point of detail fastidiously purged from everywhere else in the book.[54]

De-politicising the military and intelligence services

Striking a balance between providing independent advice and responding to the government's needs has not always been easy for the military and intelligence services. In part this is because they are inherently skewed to the right due to their Cold War origins and the shaping hand of mostly conservative federal governments over the past 50 years or so. Achieving a balance will require a fundamental shift in the perceived place of the services, both within the agencies themselves and on the part of governments. At its heart, there needs to be a genuine re-commitment to the ideal that the services exist only to serve the public good, not the government of the day.

One might hope that the military and intelligence services will automatically de-politicise somewhat with the next change of government. More likely, such a change will do little more than regenerate the existing problem, rather than bring about any sort of fundamental correction. The Labor Party is, after all, probably no less likely than the Coalition these days to try and skew the security agencies in their favour by adjusting senior appointments and playing to people's timidity and obsequiousness. There will be no shortage of security officials prepared to recalibrate their loyalty come the change of government, and anyway, the security policy settings are unlikely to change radically given the Coalition's and Labor Party's history of bipartisanship on foreign and security policy.

Against this backdrop public opinion assumes an even greater importance. In the absence of an obvious role for the judiciary (the government doesn't always break Australian laws when it perverts national security policy), public agitation remains about the only potential force for positive change, or at least reflection, in government and among the military and intelligence services.

But the public can only agitate about what it knows. This depends on the media playing a more effective role in fostering debate in Australia about the politicisation of the military and intelligence services. Too often in recent years the media has shown itself to be incompetent, lazy and compliant when it comes to security matters: incompetent, as evidenced regularly in media reports, by the obvious lack of deep understanding of security issues; lazy, as evidenced by the reluctance of many journalists to get their minds around such matters, but preparedness to publicise without scrutiny just about anything the Howard Government feeds them; and compliant, as evidenced by News Ltd's fawning support for the government over the so-called 'war on terror' and the Iraq misadventure.

If public opinion or the media lack the power to bring about change in government security policy, or to hold the government to account for its relationship with the military and intelligence services, then what or who is left to fill the gap? While the idea remains unpalatable—more so because of the trauma brought about by John Kerr's sacking of Whitlam in 1975—the only effective check on the head of government in some circumstances is currently the head of state, meaning of course the Governor-General. And, notwithstanding the potentially politicised nature of that appointment, the Governor-General could intervene, even if only to remind the Prime Minister of proper form. Whether or not Michael Jeffery, for instance, would cross Howard is not the issue here. The issue is that the Governor-General has the potential for such a moderating role.

In any case, the de-politicisation of the military and intelligence services will not be achieved until the conservative bias in the agencies is rectified, and that will not occur until there is a concerted effort to fill them with a broad range of views, from left through right. This would succeed if the change were genuinely

embraced by the agencies and formalised in relevant arrangements, for instance in the security-vetting process, workplace
agreements and in bureaucratic oversight mechanisms like the
Inspector-General of Intelligence and Security. It need not compromise the propriety of the services; remember that the dissenters
of recent years like Collins, Scrafton and Barton have all in fact
been of the traditional mould—straight, well regarded and apparently trustworthy.

Unorthodox thinking and spirited debate should be actively
encouraged in the military and intelligence services, for only in
this way might the services have a chance of out-thinking adversaries and second-guessing potential security challenges. Heads of
agencies should be encouraged to challenge the official line—out
of the public eye one would hope, but directly with the Prime
Minister when need be—when government behaviour seems to
be at odds with their know-how and any crucial information in
their possession. In such an environment officials might feel a
genuine sense of loyalty, one that would help them to deal with
unpopular orders. There would be no need for whistleblowers and
other forms of dissent. A fundamental shift is required here: that
it should not only be acceptable, but in fact desirable, to have
spirited debate, outrageous ideas and even outright argument in
the workplace. The apparatchiki in the services would do well to
keep in mind that such lateral thinking and preparedness to listen
to unexpected ideas might well have prevented the 11 September
2001 terrorist attacks in the United States.[55]

Military and intelligence officials should always be selected
and promoted on merit rather than their connections or political
reliability. So consideration should be given to prime ministers
stepping back and genuinely allowing the Public Service

Commissioner to drive the selection, promotion and appraisal, on merit, of heads of the military and intelligence agencies, unlike the current arrangement where Howard drives the process. Moreover, critical thought should be given to the suitability of the current arrangement where heads of agencies do not enjoy permanency but are encouraged to greater customer focus by the promise of performance bonuses. Such matters need to be discussed regularly, especially as they apply to organisations with unique roles.

There is also a pressing need for effective Commonwealth whistleblower legislation. All the states and the Australian Capital Territory have developed such schemes, but doing so seemingly remains beyond the federal government, despite efforts by concerned non-government law-makers to inquire into the issue and get legislation up. At a minimum, there is an urgent need for legislation to encourage and protect security officials concerned about government misconduct, and to ensure that their concerns are dealt with appropriately.

Finally, there is the need to enhance the mechanisms and processes intended to hold to account both government performance on security matters and its relationship with the military and intelligence services. Only certainty of propriety in such matters will diminish the need for dissent and encourage and protect it when it does bubble up. To that end the parliament needs to be more involved in security issues and to have the tools to do so. Parliamentarians need to commit to the need for proper debate and to vote on all significant security matters—more sitting days should be scheduled if needed. All agencies need specific legislation (DIO has none), and should table annual unclassified reports (ASIS and ONA do not).[56] And the committee system needs to be expanded and revitalised, especially as it applies to the military and intelligence services, for instance by the inclusion of minor party and independent members on the Parliamentary Joint Standing Committee on Intelligence and Security. More broadly, there also needs to be a commitment by all parliamentarians to a convention that the terms of reference for ad hoc security-related inquiries include a requirement to investigate relevant government behaviour.

Conclusion

The military and intelligence services have become increasingly politicised during the term of the Howard Government. Direct political interference and self-censorship, rather than genuine consideration of Australia's security interests, have tended to corrupt the operation of the services and have fostered compliance and timidity among their personnel.

Independent thinkers in the military and intelligence services have little room to move in this environment. The freedom they do have to voice concerns is limited to the gentlest expressions of discontent. The moment they push harder their reliability is suspect and they are sidelined or pushed out. Faced with the choice of silence or being sacked, with nothing in between, the disaffected usually default to silence.

Getting the politics out of security these days might seem to be an ambitious goal. But it is eminently achievable with a change of heart on the part of governments and the implementation of sensible reform measures. The alternative is for governments to continue to betray the trust put in them by the public, for the military and intelligence services to continue to buckle, and for the public to continue to be oblivious to it or to tolerate it. All of this may appear to be of little consequence for a while longer, but eventually the whole house of cards built up by the government could come crashing down. If so, people will die, possibly including our children and others for whom the future is shaped today by our actions and our inaction.

10

The Senate

Harry Evans

In the 2004 federal election the Coalition parties gained a one-seat majority in the Senate, taking effect on 1 July 2005. This was the first time in 24 years that a government would have such a majority, and before that it is necessary to go back to the early 1960s to find such a phenomenon. Because of the proportional representation system on which the Senate is elected, and which awards seats more nearly in proportion to votes than the single-member system of the House of Representatives, the normal situation in the Senate since the proportional system was introduced has been for no party to have a majority. This has allowed the Senate for most of its history to act with a measure of independence from the government of the day.

There was considerable apprehension about the implications of the government majority. The complacent and the partisan developed a stock phrase: 'The sky will not fall in and the sun will still rise tomorrow'. The apprehension, however, was not about celestial phenomena but the effect on the ability of the Parliament to hold the government accountable. There was a well-founded fear that a government majority would mean a decline in accountability. In the past, it was possible to believe that a government majority would not necessarily mean government control. The Fraser Government, for instance, with a majority of six from 1976 to 1981, never really controlled the Senate because there were up to twelve Coalition backbenchers who were willing to vote against the government, particularly on accountability issues, and there was therefore little fear of a major decline in accountability.

Since that time government control of its backbenchers has greatly increased. There has also been a significant concentration of power within the government in the office of the Prime Minister in recent years. The past was therefore not a good guide to likely developments. For the first ten years of the Howard Government no Coalition senator voted against it on any issue. Large hopes were held for 'rebel' National Party Senator Barnaby Joyce of Queensland, who was elected in 2004, but in the first twelve months of the government majority he voted against the government on only two bills, and one of those passed with support from other quarters. He also unsuccessfully moved, in the name of protecting small business, a motion to disallow government regulations concerning petrol retailing. One Liberal senator voted against the government legislation to overrule civil union laws in the Australian Capital Territory. Dissident backbenchers successfully rebelled over treatment of asylum seekers, and were vilified by party colleagues for their pains. These occasions were remarkable because they were unusual. The 'rebels' may soon use up their tolerable quota of rebellion. Party discipline has generally been iron-tight, particularly on accountability issues, which are not worthy of any of that precious quota.

It was also remembered that the Coalition government, before the 2004 election, showed a strong interest in gaining control of the Senate by other means, either by changing the electoral system to ensure a government majority, or by changing the Constitution to allow legislation to bypass the Senate.[1] It was very clear that the government was keen on controlling the upper house, and it was highly unlikely that the purpose of that control would be to enhance accountability.

Accountability measures

Over many years the Senate built up a structure of accountability measures designed to compel governments to explain themselves and to submit to greater scrutiny. Those measures ranged from the insistence in 1901 on appropriation bills setting out details of proposed expenditure, to the 2001 order requiring publication on the internet of details of all government contracts worth more than $100 000. All of these accountability mechanisms were made possible by lack of government control of the upper chamber, sometimes in the form of dissident government senators. For example, in 1981, during the time of the Fraser Government majority, the Senate established the Scrutiny of Bills Committee to examine and report on all legislation, using civil liberties and accountability criteria. The government opposed the establishment of the committee, but was defeated by seven of its own senators voting with the non-government parties. If the current degree of government control had applied over those years, none of the accountability measures would have come about.

The fear, in 2004, was that the Coalition Government would

use its majority to set about dismantling the accountability measures established in the past. The government had two options for doing so: simply to abolish those measures, perhaps in a disguised way (for example, by restructuring the Senate committee system); or to leave the structures in place but use its majority to ensure that they did not operate. Until mid-2006, when a restructuring of the committee system was announced, the second option was pursued, but the first option remains open to the government so long as its majority lasts.

According to classic notions of parliamentary government, the legislature imposes accountability on the executive through two main activities: legislating, if only by scrutinising and amending the legislative proposals of the executive; and inquiring into government activities and matters of public interest, partly to inform the law-making function and partly to expose government to public scrutiny, so that the public will know how they are being served.[2] Governments dislike both activities; they would prefer to pass legislation with the minimum of scrutiny and amendment, and to avoid the exposure of embarrassing mistakes or misdeeds. In recent times, governments have been able to use their tight control of lower houses, through ever-loyal party majorities, to avoid both streams of accountability in those chambers. Control of the Senate means that such avoidance can be virtually complete.

Legislation

For many years governments have had to accept that their legislation may be amended or rejected in the Senate after relatively lengthy scrutiny and debate. That situation was abruptly terminated on 1 July 2005.

Contrary to what governments would have us believe, outright rejection or obstruction of legislation has been relatively rare. In its last term without a Senate majority, the Howard Government had only seven pieces of legislation in deadlock between the two Houses, such that the simultaneous dissolution provisions of section 57 of the Constitution could have been invoked to seek to pass them. Some bills in disagreement were subsequently passed by compromise. Considering that about 150 bills are passed per year, the area of continuing disagreement was relatively small. The bills concerned were major items in the government's legislative program: partial repeal of the unfair dismissal laws, other industrial relations provisions, the full privatisation of Telstra, excision of islands from the migration zone, and changing disability entitlements. The more significant the legislation, however, the greater the scrutiny required, and the greater the requirement for support beyond the government parties which, after all, represent only 40-odd per cent of the electorate. In the end, most government legislation was passed either without amendment or after compromise over amendments.

Now, however, it is clear that government legislation will be passed only in the form the government wants, and that non-government amendments will not be allowed, even where amendments have been supported in principle by Coalition back-benchers.

The change is illustrated by before-and-after examples of the treatment of two pieces of related legislation. The government's first major anti-terrorism bill, the Australian Security Intelligence Organisation Amendment (Terrorism) Bill 2002, was passed only after extensive scrutiny and amendment in the Senate, and compromise over many of the amendments. This treatment of the legislation was widely praised as ensuring that basic civil liberties were not fatally undermined and that the government's more draconian proposals were not passed. In 2006, however, the Telecommunications Interception Amendment Bill, greatly expanding the power of law enforcement agencies to intercept and access electronic communications, was passed after the rejection of all non-government amendments, including amendments for which government backbenchers had expressed support during committee examination of the bill.

The same situation occurred with the Anti-Terrorism Bill (No. 2) 2005, which introduced for the first time detention without charge. Some government amendments to that bill were said to allay some concerns of government backbenchers, but other amendments for which they had expressed support were rejected. Even that degree of concession has now apparently disappeared. A package of fuel tax bills was passed unamended in June 2006 despite government senators on a committee recommending that it not pass until outstanding issues were resolved and other government senators expressing discontent with it. The government controls the legislative process and is able to get whatever it wants in the way of law-making.

The Senate chamber is not the only forum for scrutinising legislation. The system of subjecting bills to scrutiny in committees, including by hearing evidence from interested organisations and members of the public, was established by the Senate over many years to enhance government accountability for legislative proposals. This system is still in place, but the Coalition Government has used its majority to restrict the time available for committees to examine bills. The average time allotted declined from 40 to 28 days, which gives potential witnesses less time to prepare their submissions and to make their contributions in oral evidence. The government has also blocked the referral of some bills to committees. And the committees cannot amend bills, so their evidence and reports can simply be ignored, even when government members of the committees have expressed their support for changes to legislation, as the examples referred to indicate.

The Coalition Government also now has the ability to force legislation through the chamber by means of the gag (the termination of debate) and guillotine (the limitation of time for the consideration of a bill). The guillotine was used in periods of non-government majorities when the government could gain the support of other parties to set time limits for debate. Very often, these were 'civilised guillotines', in which the time limits were negotiated between parties. On one occasion, the Leader of the Opposition in the Senate moved the motion specifying the allotted times. Now the government has exclusive power to determine how much time will be allowed for debate, and has used that power on several occasions. From 1 January 2004 to 30 June 2005 there were no gag motions and only one guillotine; from 1 July 2005 to 30 June 2006 there were sixteen and five, respectively. The times allotted for major bills were less than those for bills of comparable importance in the past. The Anti-Terrorism Bill (No. 2) 2005 was given only six hours, the highly contentious Welfare to Work legislation only seven hours, and the Radioactive Waste Management Bill three hours. By way of contrast, the Native Title Bill 1993 was considered for 50 hours with a 'civilised guillotine', and the Workplace Relations Bill 1996 for 49 hours.

A government with control over law-making has the power to alter the electoral law to favour its own re-election. The temptation is irresistible. A piece of electoral legislation passed in June 2006, shortening times for enrolment and increasing the limit on non-disclosable donations to parties, was seen by the non-government parties as the first instalment of such a project.

The number of days of meeting has declined. In 2003 the Senate sat on 64 days, in 2005 on 57 (the 2004 sittings were shortened by the election). From 1 January to 30 June 2006 there were only 22 sitting days. This means that there is less time for non-government parties to devote to legislation and to exercise the accountability mechanisms available to them.

Inquiries

Until announcing a restructuring in June 2006, not implemented at the time of writing, the government had left in place the structure of the Senate committee system. Under the existing system half of the subject-specialised standing committees have non-government majorities and non-government chairs. These committees, called references committees, were designed to inquire into matters referred to them by the Senate. The government, however, used its majority to control the matters referred to the committees for inquiry. It is clear that no inquiries will be allowed into matters that might expose dubious government activities.

Before 1 July 2005, for example, there were inquiries by references committees into the government's industrial relations advertising campaign, whereby $55 million of public funds were spent on advertising government proposals which had not even been *introduced* into Parliament, much less passed, and into the Regional Partnerships and Sustainable Regions Programs, under which millions of dollars in grants were given to private organisations and individuals for regional development projects, some of a dubious nature. In both cases, money had not been specifically appropriated for the purposes of the expenditure.

It is unlikely that any such inquiries will be allowed in the future. Since July 2005, proposals for a range of inquiries in the Senate have been rejected by the government majority. These include proposed references to the references committees on the aviation safety regime and refugees and visa-holders which were rejected by the government on 2 March 2006, when Coalition senators voted against the references in spite of some having expressed disquiet about the aviation safety issue. No ministers or government senators spoke to the motions, leading to charges of contempt for the committee system. In spite of that criticism, the same situation recurred, for example on 22 June 2006, when a proposed reference on the practical operation of welfare to work regulations was rejected with no reasons given. It is now expected that, if the committees are given any work to do, they will be like the House of Representatives committees, examining only matters referred to them, or approved, by ministers.

A lack of government cooperation with other inquiry processes has been evident. In the past the Senate has used orders for the production of documents as a major inquiry mechanism and information resource. Motions were passed requiring ministers to present to the Senate, or to Senate committees, documents about specified matters of public interest. If the government refused to produce documents in response to an order, the Senate could take other measures, such as committee hearings, to gain the required information, or impose procedural penalties, such as postponement of legislation, on the government. Even before gaining its majority, the government was building up a record of refusals to produce documents in response to Senate orders. Going back to just before the change of government, in the Parliament of 1993–96, 53 such orders were made, all but four being complied with. In the Parliament of 1996–98, 48 orders were made and five were not complied with. In the Parliament of 1998–2001, there were 56 orders, and fifteen not complied with, and in that of 2002–04, 89 orders with 46 not complied with. Since 1 July 2005 only one motion for production of documents has been agreed to. All others have been rejected.

For example, five motions for the production of documents were rejected by the government on 17 August 2005. A ministerial statement offered various grounds for refusing to produce the documents: the 'longstanding convention' that legal advice to government is not produced (this cannot be true because of the many past occasions on which supportive advices have been voluntarily produced by government); the documents were Cabinet documents (this ground is supposed to be confined to disclosing the deliberations of Cabinet, not every document having a connection to Cabinet); and the document concerned was 'not intended for public disclosure' (if a document *is* intended for public disclosure, presumably it would be disclosed and then there would be no point in calling for it). The view of the government is that 'requests' for documents should be made directly to ministers' offices but, even if such requests are met, this has the disadvantage that the documents are not tabled in the Senate and so their publication is not given the status of proceedings in Parliament.

A similar approach has been taken to requests by committees for information. A report on 13 October 2005 by the Finance and Public Administration References Committee on works on the Gallipoli Peninsula, a matter referred to it before 1 July 2005, reported the refusal of the government to provide relevant legal advices supplied to the government. This material disclosed a very large expansion of the grounds for refusal to provide such documents. At first the Department of Foreign Affairs and Trade attempted to argue that the documents could not be provided because Senate Standing Order 73 prohibits the asking of questions seeking legal opinions at question time. It was pointed out that this has nothing to do with the provision of documents to committees, that legal advices to government have often been provided in the past, and that under past Senate resolutions refusals to provide documents should be based on a ministerial claim of public interest immunity on specified grounds. The department then stated that the minister had refused to provide the material because of 'a longstanding practice accepted by successive Australian governments not to disclose legal advice which has been provided to government, unless there are compelling reasons to do so in a particular case'. It was pointed out that this 'longstanding practice' had in fact never been advanced before, and would have prevented most of the cases of disclosure of legal advice that had occurred in the past. The response to this was simply a reassertion of the 'longstanding practice'.[3]

More recently there has been a tendency not to give any reasons at all for refusals to provide information. Following the 17 August 2005 episode, six motions for documents were rejected without any reasons given. If this lack of cooperation continues senators may just give up moving these motions.

Estimates hearings

In the past the major accountability mechanism of the Senate has been the estimates hearings. From their beginning in 1970 estimates hearings were an opportunity to question ministers and officers about any activity of government departments and agencies. They were a general inquisition into the operations of government. Both Labor and Coalition governments have made the claim that when they were in opposition estimates hearings were confined to the estimates (questions about how much money would be spent on particular purposes), and that since they gained office the hearings have been debauched from this pure purpose, such that the committees should be brought back to their original function. This is not true; the hearings have always ranged over any and all government activities.

In 1999 there appeared to be a concerted effort by ministers to restrict the estimates hearings to their claimed original purpose by declining to answer questions which were not about how much money was to be spent on particular functions. This led to a dispute which found its way into the Senate, to the Procedure Committee and back to the Senate again. The Senate adopted the report of the Procedure Committee, to the effect that all questions going to the operations and financial positions of government departments and agencies are relevant questions for estimates hearings. As the Procedure Committee made clear, this only reasserted what had always been the practice. In more recent times, when ministers and chairs of committees have indicated impatience with lines of questioning they have been reminded of the 1999 resolution. In some cases they have been invited to move a motion in the Senate for the repeal of the 1999 resolution if they consider that the practice should be changed. So far this invitation has not been taken up, but the possibility now cannot be disregarded.

The 1999 incident also demonstrates an important aspect of the change brought about by the government majority. If a Senate committee encounters resistance to its inquiries, it can only report the matter to the Senate and it is then for the Senate to provide a remedy. In the past, where ministers have resisted inquiries in committees, the majority of the Senate has undertaken various steps to pursue the inquiries, including directing committees to meet again, directing particular witnesses to appear, instructing committees to conduct wider inquiries, ordering ministers to produce particular information and extending the length of question time in the chamber. These measures have the effect of raising the level of any dispute, and have generally been successful. In effect, if a government wished to be uncooperative it had to get into a major fight in the chamber, with the potential to disrupt its legislative program. This ability of the Senate to impose a remedy has effectively been removed because of government control from 1 July 2005.

The value of estimates hearings in improving accountability and probity of government has long been widely recognised. The hearings allow apparent problems in government operations to be explored and exposed, and give rise to a large amount of information which would not otherwise be disclosed. It is often said that estimates hearings are largely devoted to party politics, with non-government senators attempting to put blame on ministers or particular officers and to win political points. This should not be a matter for reproach, and nor does it invalidate the hearings as an accountability process. Free states work through party politics.

The ultimate safeguard against the misuse of power by a government is the ability of its opponents and rivals to find out about, and draw attention to, its mistakes and misdeeds. Accountability is not a refined process which operates on an elevated plane, above sordid politics. Accountability operates in the realm of politics.

The effect of the government control of the Senate was well demonstrated by the treatment in the February 2006 estimates hearings of the Australian Wheat Board (AWB) Iraq wheat bribery affair. The hearings began with a declaration by the government that it had instructed all officers not to answer any questions about the matter. The only reason given was that it would be undesirable to have Senate committees looking at the affair while the Cole commission of inquiry was conducting its examination. It was explicitly stated that this was not a public interest immunity claim, that is, a claim that answering questions would be harmful to the public interest in some specific way. It was simply a refusal to answer.

This was contrary to past Senate resolutions, which declared that ministerial claims to be excused from answering questions in Senate inquiries should be based on particular public interest grounds, and the claims would be considered and determined by the Senate. In the past, matters before commissions of inquiry were the subject of debate and questioning; such commissions are not courts and there is no question of the sub judice principle applying. Had the government's declaration been made before 1 July 2005 it is fairly certain that some action in the Senate would have followed. After its majority took effect the government was able to make its declaration secure in the knowledge that the majority of the Senate would not take any remedial action.

It might be thought that this episode did not disclose an

accountability gap, because the Cole commission would be pursuing its inquiry. The most significant point about the Cole commission, however, is that it came about because of pressure from powerful bodies overseas, ironically starting with members of another legislature freer than our own, the US Congress, and flowing through the United Nations and its inquiries. Without that overseas pressure a great deal of information about the matter would never have been disclosed, if the whole affair had become known at all. The accountability gap will be of greater concern in cases where such an external element is not present, the government is not forced to conduct its own inquiry, and the last remaining parliamentary avenue of inquiries, the estimates hearings, are frustrated.

The AWB matter could well be a model for further refusals to provide particular information in the estimates hearings, with no possibility of any remedy. It was unprecedented in that an inquiry by a government-appointed commission had not previously been the basis for a general direction to officers not to provide information. There had been previous occasions of particular refusals to answer questions on various grounds, and of reluctance to answer questions because of other inquiries, but no general direction on that ground. It was a significant extension of past claims.

During the estimates hearings many questions are taken on notice by ministers or officers or placed on notice by senators. The committees are required by the Senate's procedures to set deadlines for answering questions on notice. To encourage ministers and departments not to ignore the deadlines, the Senate has a procedure known as the 30-day rule. If answers are 30 days or more overdue, any senator can ask for an explanation in the chamber and initiate a debate. This potentially imposes a penalty of loss of legislating time. The procedure provides no remedy, however, against flat refusals to answer questions. The Senate now cannot impose any more effective remedy. The procedure is therefore not a significant disincentive for refusals to answer.

It has been suggested that more questions are now taken on notice and that fewer answers are provided, and more slowly provided, because ministers know that no more effective remedy can be taken in the chamber. Statistics have not been collected for a sufficient time to test this suggestion, but it appears that the practices of delaying answers to questions on notice and simply not answering them or providing non-responsive answers have become more common.

On 11 May 2006 the government passed a motion which had the effect of stripping two days from the time allotted for the main budget estimates hearings later that month. This may be the beginning of a winding back of the hearings. The May 2006 hearings were marked by several significant refusals to answer questions, and by responses to the effect that answering some questions would be too expensive. This placing of a price on accountability may be the beginning of a move to ration it.

The weakening of the estimates hearings as an accountability mechanism was illustrated by a motion in the Senate on 8 February 2006 to require Managing Director of Telstra Mr Sol Trujillo to appear in an estimates hearing to explain his administration of the government-majority-owned communications carrier. The motion was rejected, although Coalition senators had earlier said that Mr Trujillo should appear. Apparently they were pacified by an offer of a private briefing by him, again illustrating the government's control over when and how it will be accountable, if at all.

Effect on public service

Estimates hearings provide public servants with an opportunity to demonstrate their professionalism and to show how effectively they carry out their functions. In particular, they should be able to show that they have performed the role appropriate to public servants, of advising ministers and carrying out both ministerial and departmental decisions with legality and propriety. Difficulties arise when public servants are seen to be doing whatever ministers want and then helping to conceal illegalities or improprieties.

The inability of the Senate to pursue remedies for ministerial refusals to provide information, apart from posing a danger to accountability of government, also gives rise to a danger for public servants. It potentially deprives them of the opportunity to demonstrate their professionalism and capacity. It also removes a safeguard for public servants. Over many years reference has been made to the 'estimates test': if a person responsible for some government activity would not feel comfortable in defending that activity in the estimates hearings, then there is probably something wrong with the activity. Officers can use the test to check for themselves the operations in which they are engaged, but may also use it to deflect improper or inappropriate demands made upon them by the political wing of government, ministers and their ministerial staff. The political wing could be told that, while officers would provide appropriate assistance, they would also be obliged to explain their role at the next round of estimates hearings, and that ministers would have to take responsibility for explaining any politically based decisions and actions of dubious propriety. The estimates test is now seriously weakened because government does not need to worry about the Senate, and public servants may be told not to worry about the Senate either, and to get on and carry out their instructions.

Financial control

This undermining of the estimates scrutiny process has occurred in the context of a significant decline in parliamentary control of expenditure under the financial system put in place by the government since 1997. By a series of legislative changes supposedly of a technical accounting character, public finance has been transformed. In theory, and in accordance with the Constitution, Parliament annually appropriates money for specified purposes of government. Now, in practice, most government expenditure is funded from sources of money which are not annually subject to parliamentary approval. In the annual appropriations, money is allocated to outcomes which are so nebulous and vaguely expressed that the money can be spent on anything. For example, $3 billion was appropriated to the Department of Employment and Workplace Relations for 'higher productivity, high pay workplaces', a propaganda description which allowed $55 million to be spent on advertising the government's Work Choices legislation before it had appeared. In approving such appropriations the Parliament is given no guarantees on what the money might be spent on.

A challenge was mounted in the High Court on the basis that the government's advertising campaign was not an authorised purpose of expenditure under the appropriations made by the Parliament for the Department of Employment and Workplace Relations. The majority judgment, in rejecting this claim, confirmed that appropriations are now a blank cheque, and the court will not correct this situation. It is Parliament's responsibility to ensure that expenditure is appropriate. The joint judgment of the majority was accurately characterised by dissenting Justice McHugh as authorising an agency 'to spend money on whatever outputs it pleases'.[4] Justices McHugh and Kirby, in the minority, pointed out that the majority repudiated the principle on which earlier judgments of the court were based, that expenditure was confined to the purpose specified by Parliament in the appropriation. The separate judgment of Chief Justice Gleeson explicitly put the responsibility for control of expenditure back on to the Parliament:

> If Parliament formulates the purposes of appropriation in broad, general terms, then those terms must be applied with the breadth and generality they bear.[5]

In other words, if Parliament makes appropriations with vague descriptions of their purpose, it is Parliament's problem. Chief Justice Gleeson helpfully indicated what must be done:

> The higher the level of abstraction, or the greater the scope for political interpretation, involved in a proposed outcome appropriation, the greater may be the detail required by Parliament before appropriating a sum to such a purpose; and the greater may be the scrutiny involved in a review of such expenditure after it has occurred.[6]

The heavy responsibility resting on the Parliament to exert this kind of proper control and scrutiny over expenditure is now even less likely to be met with the government controlling the Senate. (Surprisingly, the Finance and Public Administration References Committee initiated, and succeeded in having passed, a reference to itself on the financial system, but this does not increase the chances of any changes.) The consequent ability of the government to spend as much money as it likes on whatever it likes greatly increases its power to keep itself in office, to reward obedience and to punish dissent.

Question time

Question time is the only part of parliamentary proceedings most people ever see, but is virtually useless as a forum of parliamentary inquiry and accountability. Notoriously, ministers are able to avoid answering non-government questions, while responding to government backbenchers' questions, prepared in ministerial offices, with barrages of propaganda.

Even this occasion has been significantly weakened by the Coalition majority in the Senate. At the first sittings after 1 July 2005, the allocation of questions between the parties, which had in the past been determined by agreement between the parties, was changed by the government to give itself the great bulk of the time devoted to questions and answers.

The 30-day rule also applies to questions placed on notice in the Senate, but is also not an effective remedy against simple ministerial refusals to answer.

In April 2003 a senator sent a letter to the Leader of the Government in the Senate, asking him about procedures adopted by the government to determine whether it will release documents to the Senate. Having received no reply, in 2004 the senator put a question on notice asking when the minister would respond to her letter. The letter and the question remained unanswered at the general election of 2004, so in the next Parliament she placed the question on notice again. On two occasions she used the 30-day procedure to ask in the chamber for an explanation of the failure to answer the question and the letter; on neither occasion did she receive either an explanation or an answer, except an off-the-cuff response in June 2005 when she summarised the letter. The Leader of the Government in the Senate retired in March 2006, with the question and the letter still unanswered, and the question was then redirected to the incoming Leader of the Government. Finally, in May 2006 the new minister responded that 'requests' for information would be considered on their merits. This is an extreme case, but differs from the general recent response pattern only in degree.

Integrity of processes

At one point it appeared that the government's majority had been used to threaten the very integrity of Senate inquiries.

The President (Tasmanian Liberal Senator Paul Calvert) made a determination under the relevant standing order on 5 September 2005 according precedence to a motion to refer to the Privileges Committee a matter raised by the Finance and Public Administration References Committee. The matter involved evidence given by a mayor in the course of the committee's inquiry into Regional Partnership Program grants. The committee had evidence suggesting that the mayor's statements were untrue, and the committee was not satisfied with an explanation which he subsequently provided. Normally, motions to refer matters to the Privileges Committee are passed without debate following the President's determination. It was the intention of procedures for dealing with privilege matters adopted in 1988 to take them out of partisan controversy. The person concerned in this matter, however, was a member of the Liberal Party, and the government apparently decided to use its majority to reject the motion to refer the matter to the Privileges Committee.

The chair of that committee, Senator Faulkner, stated that this was a 'degrading' of the non-partisan method for dealing with privilege matters. A government senator stated in debate that there ought to be a prima facie case before the reference was made, but the procedures of 1988 were deliberately designed to avoid any judgment about a prima facie case.[7] The failure to refer the privilege matter to the Privileges Committee, unfortunate from an accountability view, may also have sent a message that committees may safely be trifled with if the trifler is of the right political allegiance.

Subsequently, it was put to the President in an estimates hearing for the Department of the Senate that he should adopt a process to ensure that privilege matters to which he gives precedence are referred to the Privileges Committee without debate and votes based on partisan considerations. The President accepted this suggestion. No further privilege cases have arisen so far to test the process.

Accountability in decline

The government majority in the Senate has greatly increased the ability of the government to do what it likes and not to explain itself except to the extent it chooses. The information available to the public on the performance of the government is now limited virtually to that which the government itself chooses to disclose. The accountability of government to the Parliament and the public, and the ability of would-be critics and dissenters to find out what is really going on, has been significantly reduced.

It is unrealistic to expect an investigative media to perform the role of a hobbled Senate. Many people, especially public office-bearers, will not talk except in a protected forum. Only the parliamentary forum can offer the protection of parliamentary privilege if, of course, it is allowed by government to have something to protect.

It would be unwise for supporters of accountability simply to wait until the electors change the situation. They should keep on raising accountability issues and vigorously pursue, by debate and by publication, every move to weaken the accountability procedures and processes which have been painstakingly built up over so many years by their predecessors.

Signs of resistance

Sarah Maddison and Clive Hamilton

This book has documented an alarming decline in the health of Australian democracy over the last decade, one reflecting a growing authoritarianism in Canberra. The evidence shows that the Howard Government's intolerance and silencing strategies are not confined to organisations that might be seen as its political enemies but extend to all of the institutions that make up a democratic political system.

Much of the government's activity in this regard has been 'beneath the radar' of most Australians, yet the effects of these strategies are disturbing to say the least, and the long-term implications are deeply worrying. However, these chapters also reveal that there are signs of resistance to this creeping authoritarianism. History shows that autocrats must always confront the popular demand for self-determination. Any government of a democratic nation that sets out to erode its essential institutions and practices will inevitably sow the seeds of its own downfall. Growing numbers, committed to genuine democratic participation and disturbed by their government's authoritarian tendencies, will resist anti-democratic policies and practices and will stand up to bullying tactics even at great personal cost. Such a trend is becoming evident in Australia.

Chapter 2 of this book outlines a number of criteria for the assessment of democracy, as employed by the Democratic Audit of Australia team, including popular control of public decision-making, political equality in exercising that control, protection of human rights and civil liberties, and the quality of public debate. In considering the developing signs of resistance to the Howard Government's anti-democratic tendencies we can observe a degree of public endorsement of these principles.

Signs of resistance are evident in the parliament itself. Despite a reputation for unprecedented levels of party discipline, Prime Minister Howard faced parliamentary revolt over legislation considered by dissidents in the party to be unjust. The most notable of these is perhaps the August 2006 revolt over the proposed Migration Amendment (Designated Unauthorised Arrivals) Bill, which would have seen asylum claims by all unauthorised arrivals processed offshore and asylum seekers held on Nauru until their claims were finalised. The Bill was widely regarded as an attempt to appease the Indonesian Government, which had expressed annoyance at Australia's decision to accept as refugees a group of West Papuan asylum seekers who had arrived by boat in January 2006. Citing the unfairness and potential for harm in the Bill's provisions, two government MPs, Petro Georgiou and Russell Broadbent, crossed the floor to vote against the government. A third, Judi Moylan, abstained from voting. Speaking against the Bill in parliament, Broadbent acknowledged the potential risk to his career that his actions would provoke in the government, but expressed his determination to uphold democratic principles.

> I believe there is a potential for this bill to cause serious harm to the progress we have made on this issue as a nation and to the vulnerable people it would affect. I will be voting against these amendments knowing that there are some in my party who do not agree with the 'plural tradition' of the Liberal Party and its principles of free thought and individual conscience. Some warn that any dissent is a form of political death . . . It is not the office of the federal member that is important; it is what you do when in office. I take comfort in the words of Dr Martin Luther King, 'The ultimate measure of a man is not where he stands in moments of comfort and convenience, but where he stands at times of challenge and controversy.' [1]

Moylan cited other aspects of democratic principle and practice in her speech where she claimed the Bill's provisions would place asylum seekers 'out of range of Australian public scrutiny and support' in a manner contrary to the principle of the rule of law. The rule of law, Moylan claimed, 'is the foundation of democracy. It requires as a minimum access to judicial review of administrative action, the right to a fair trial, the right to private communications with a lawyer and access to the courts. This Bill removes or diminishes those rights'.[2] Although the Bill was still passed in the House of Representatives, the Prime Minister was forced to abandon it before it entered the Senate when it became clear that this dissent would not allow it to be passed there.

Outside the parliament, more signs of dissent can be found. In late August 2006 the chemical weapons expert and former diplomat Dr John Gee went public with details of the government's suppression of advice concerning the existence of weapons of mass destruction (WMD) in Iraq. Gee released his letter of resignation from the US-led Iraq Survey Group, which he had sent to the Department of Foreign Affairs and Trade in March 2004. Gee had outlined his complete lack of confidence in 'the integrity of the process' involved in the hunt for WMD in Iraq, and expressed his concern that reports to the Australian Government withheld important information and were used to justify earlier judgements rather than establish the facts on the ground in Iraq. Gee also released a series of emails outlining his efforts to stimulate government officials, including Foreign Affairs Minister Alexander Downer, to act on his allegations. The emails, which Downer has since labelled 'a conspiracy theory', in fact reveal the government's reluctance to even acknowledge Gee's claims, much less do anything about them. Gee's claims have been backed by his former colleague Rod Barton, whose own attempt to expose flaws in the search for WMD is detailed in Chapter 9. As journalist Marian Wilkinson observed, Gee's case 'highlights the chronic reluctance of the Howard government to receive frank and fearless advice and the dwindling number of public servants willing to provide it'.[3] That Gee, like Barton and Andrew Wilkie, was prepared to resign for his principles in the first instance and later expose the government's failure to act demonstrates a considerable degree of courage.

Other examples of this type of resistance to the silencing regime are increasingly coming to light. Among them are rejections of perceived injustices, as evident in the decision by several charitable NGOs—including Catholic Welfare Australia, the St Vincent de Paul Society and the Uniting Church—to pull out of the government's controversial welfare-to-work reforms.[4] The new program, which would see sole parents and those on disability pensions stripped of benefits for eight weeks should they fail to comply with onerous work tests, were described as 'dangerous' and 'humiliating' by some charities that had previously enjoyed favoured status from the government, such as the Salvation Army. Several charities refused to take up, or later withdrew, from contracts to provide the financial case management services required under the new provisions for fear of compromising their relationships with vulnerable clients.[5] For these charities, the democratic principle was one of fairness and social justice.

Another notable dissenter is Defence Force chief Angus Houston. Although as Air Force chief in 2004 Air Marshall Houston gave evidence to the Senate inquiry contradicting the Howard Government's claims that children had been thrown overboard by asylum seekers, Houston was the obvious candidate to succeed General Peter Cosgrove as Defence Chief in 2005. In September 2006 Houston criticised Defence Minister Brendan Nelson's public statements concerning the death in Iraq of Private Jake Kovko. Directly contradicting Nelson's claims that he had merely repeated what he had been told by Houston, the Defence chief declared that he had repeatedly told the minister not to say anything until the circumstances of Kovko's death were known.[6] Houston took a risk to defend the principle of truth in government.

Each of these examples demonstrates the triumph of conscience over fear. In the face of a government that has repeatedly pilloried individuals for speaking out, or for just doing their job, these actions take courage and a determination to let principle prevail regardless of the personal, professional or organisational consequences. Australians have always applauded courageous individuals and organisations who have spoken out about wrongdoing or merely expressed an alternative point of view. The dissenters know they will be criticised, smeared and even vilified and their organisations may lose funding or status. The pages of this book testify to the fact that these fears are well founded. But the success of the Howard Government in controlling public opinion and stifling debate has only been possible because of the failure of heart of many others who could and should speak up regardless of the personal consequences.

Democracy needs champions. Australian political culture has declined to the point where speaking up is the exception and remaining quiet is the norm. Dissenters have been recast as 'out-of-touch elites', 'Howard haters', or rogue individuals with an axe to grind, allowing dissenting and independent opinion to be routinely suppressed in the name of unity and stability. By contrast, a vibrant democracy must embrace variety of opinion and encourage active engagement of institutions that are comprised of and are accountable to the people themselves. Without that engagement and participation of citizens democracy is dead. Around the world people are struggling to free themselves from authoritarian rule and develop democratic systems of government that rest on the authority of the people themselves. In Australia our own fear and complacency are allowing these same institutions to be ground down.

Democracy is a noble ideal, a prize for those prepared to promote and defend it. When democratic institutions are eroded authoritarianism is not far behind. In light of this, it is time to reassert the role of dissent and to praise the contribution to democracy made by those who speak out, engage in debate and criticise the powerful, no matter how uncomfortable it may make the government of the day. Dissenters should not be silenced or pilloried; as defenders of Australian democracy they deserve our gratitude.

Notes

1. Dissent in Australia

1   Senate Privileges Committee, 124th Report—person referred to in the Senate: Professor David Peetz, 6 December 2005, <http://www.aph.gov.au/senate/committee/priv_ctte/report_124/index.htm>.

2   Senate Privileges Committee, 126th Report—person referred to in the Senate: Professor Barbara Pocock, 27 February 2006, <http://www.aph.gov.au/senate/committee/priv_ctte/report_126/index.htm>.

3   Senate Finance and Public Administration Committee, report of the inquiry into government advertising and accountability, December 2005, <http://www.aph.gov.au/senate/committee/fapa_ctte/govtadvertising/report/index.htm>.

4   Senate Finance and Public Administration Committee. The committee noted: 'The Committee is aware of ongoing attacks upon Dr Young by Senator Abetz's staffer, Peter Phelps, in www.crikey.com.au.'

5 Eric Abetz, 'Electoral reform: making our democracy fairer for all', speech to the Sydney Institute, 4 October 2005.

6 ibid.

7 Thanks are due to Andrew Macintosh for providing the material on Justice Kirby.

8 Andrew Clark, 'Untold Power', *Australian Financial Review*, 23 March 2002.

9 Senate Hansard, Commonwealth of Australia, 12 March 2002, pp. 573–7.

10 E. Sidoti, 'Australian democracy: challenging the rise of contemporary authoritarianism', An occasional paper published by Catholics in Coalition for Justice and Peace, Sydney, 2003, p. 32.

11 ibid., p. 32.

12 J. Walter, 'Why Howard goes too far: institutional change and the renaissance of groupthink', refereed paper presented to the Australasian Political Studies Association Conference, University of Adelaide, Adelaide, 29 September to 1 October 2004, p. 20.

13 A. West, 'Federal Politics/Media: A Right-Wing Conspiracy', NewMatilda.com 19 July 2006, <http://www.newmatilda.com/home/articledetail.asp?ArticleID=1692&CategoryID=>.

14 A. Gutmann and D. Thompson, *Why Deliberative Democracy?*, Princeton University Press, Princeton, 2004, p. 45.

15 C. Kayrooz, P. Kinnear and P. Preston, 'Academic Freedom and Commercialisation of Australian Universities', Discussion Paper No. 37, The Australia Institute, Canberra, March 2001.

16 ibid., p. 37.

17 Leigh Dayton, 'Media management spins out of control', *The Australian*, Higher Education supplement, 3 May 2006, p. 26.

18 CSIRO Media Liaison Group, 'Contribution to Bureau Annual Report 1984–85', CSIRO, Canberra, 1985.

19 ABC, 'FTA may pose risk to blood donation safety standards', *PM*, 14 July 2006, <www.abc.net/pm/content/2006/s1687267.htm>.

20 Piers Ackerman, 'Fighting to keep our shores safe and clean', *Daily Telegraph*, 27 April 2006.

21 ABC Online, 'Academics branded "anti-US" over FTA research', 29 July 2006. This report implied that the federal government had attempted to silence the researchers. Chubb has said that the calls he received were not from the government but from unspecified others.

22 Personal communication.

23 The role of these two and others are detailed by David Marr and Marian Wilkinson in *Dark Victory*, Allen & Unwin, Sydney, 2003.

24 ibid., pp. 256–7.

25 P.P. McGuinness, 'No wind of change at the ABC', *The Australian*, 19 June 2006.

26 Australian Broadcasting Corporation, 'Publishing plans scrapped', *Lateline*, ABC Television, 29 June 2006, <www.abc.net.au/lateline/content/2006/s1675156.htm>.

27 See David Marr, 'Theatre Under Howard', The Philip Parsons Memorial Lecture, 9 October 2005, Sydney, from which this material is drawn.

2. Redefining democracy

1 G. Maddox, *Australian Democracy in Theory and Practice*, 5th edition, Pearson Longman, Sydney, 2005, p. 2.

2 ibid., p. 45.

3 ibid., p. 2.

4 ibid., p. 4; H.V. Emy and O.E. Hughes, *Australian Politics: Realities in conflict*, Macmillan, Melbourne, 1991, p. 226.

5 Maddox, *Australian Democracy*, p. 42.

6 For more information see the IDEA website at: <http://www.idea.int/democracy/index.cfm>.

7 For a detailed discussion of these principles see M. Sawer, 'Audit values: Reflecting the complexity of representative democracy', Democratic Audit of Australia, 2005, http://democratic.audit.anu.edu.au>.

8   Maddox, *Australian Democracy*, p. 43; IDEA website: <http://www.idea.int/democracy/index.cfm>.

9   S. Macedo et al., *Democracy at Risk: How political choices undermine citizen participation, and what we can do about it*, Brookings Institution Press, Washington, 2005.

10 ibid., p. 4.

11 S. Maddison and R. Denniss, 'Democratic constraint and embrace: implications for progressive non-government advocacy organisations in Australia', *Australian Journal of Political Science*, vol. 40, no. 3, 2005.

12 J. Dryzek, *Deliberative Democracy and Beyond: Liberals, critics, contestations*, Oxford University Press, Oxford, 2000, p. 29.

13 Emy and Hughes, *Australian Politics*, p. 235.

14 B. Hindess, 'Deficit by Design', *Australian Journal of Public Administration*, vol. 61, no. 1, 2002, p. 3.

15 R. Melville, *Changing roles of community-sector peak bodies in a neo-liberal policy environment in Australia*, an ARC-funded study, Institute of Social Change and Critical Inquiry, Faculty of Arts, University of Wollongong, 2003, p. 108.

16 Maddox, *Australian Democracy*, p. 11.

17 M. Latham, *The Latham Diaries*, Melbourne University Press, Melbourne, 2005; C. Hamilton, 'What's left? The death of social democracy', *Quarterly Essay 21*, Black Inc., Melbourne, 2006.

18 H. Lasswell quoted in Maddox, *Australian Democracy*, p. 29.

19 M. Sawer, 'Governing for the Mainstream: Implications for Community Representation', *Australian Journal of Public Administration*, vol. 61, no. 1, 2002, pp. 39–49; C. Johnson, *Governing Change: From Keating to Howard*, University of Queensland Press in association with the API Network, Brisbane, 2000.

20 Maddox, *Australian Democracy*, p. 460.

21 Emy and Hughes, *Australian Politics*, p. 236.

22 ibid.

23 Dryzek, *Deliberative Democracy and Beyond*, pp. 31–2.

24 Emy and Hughes, *Australian Politics*, p. 237.

25 Maddox, *Australian Democracy*, p. 489.

26 S. Brenton, 'Public confidence in Australian democracy', Democratic Audit of Australia, 2005, <http://democratic.audit.anu.edu.au>.

27 The Power Inquiry, *Power to the people: The report of Power, an independent inquiry into Britain's democracy*, March 2006, <http://www.powerinquiry.org>, p. 35.

28 A. Gutmann and D. Thompson, *Why Deliberative Democracy?*, Princeton University Press, Princeton, 2004, p. 55.

29 J. Walter, 'Why Howard goes too far: institutional change and the renaissance of groupthink', refereed paper presented to the Australasian Political Studies Association Conference, University of Adelaide, Adelaide, 29 September to 1 October 2004, p. 22.

30 J. Kane and P. Bishop, 'Consultation and contest: the danger of mixing modes', *Australian Journal of Public Administration*, vol. 61, no. 1, 2002, p. 88.

31 M. Rawsthorne, 2004, 'Government/Non-government partnerships: Towards deliberative democracy in policy making?', a discussion paper for the Western Sydney Community Forum, Inc., 2004, p. 5.

32 Maddox, *Australian Democracy*, p. 32.

33 J. Howard, 'The Party of ideas', *The Party Room*, 1, Winter, 2005, p. 5.

34 L. Carson, 'Citizens and governments: stroppy adversaries or partners in deliberation?', *Australian Review of Public Affairs*, April 2005, <http://www.australianreview.net/digest/2005/04/carson.html>.

35 Maddox, *Australian Democracy*, p. 492.

36 ibid., p. 38.

37 Gutmann and Thompson, *Why Deliberative Democracy?*, p. 44.

38 ibid., p. 41.

39 J. Uhr, *Deliberative Democracy in Australia: The changing place of parliament*, Cambridge University Press, Melbourne, 1998, p. 10.

40 Gutmann and Thompson, *Why Deliberative Democracy?*, p. 41.

41   ibid., p. 30.

42   F. Fischer, *Reframing Public Policy: Discursive politics and deliberative practices*, Oxford University Press, Oxford, 2003, p. 205.

43   J. Waterford, 'Accountability: By all accounts this is a government that can get away with anything', *Australian Policy Online*, 5 July 2006, <http://www.apo.org.au>.

44   Maddox, *Australian Democracy*, pp. 43–4.

3. Universities

1   A. Bolt, 'Grants to grumble', *Herald-Sun*, 19 November 2003.

2   G. Haigh, 'The Nelson touch', *The Monthly*, May 2006, pp. 21–2.

3   A. Bolt, 'Paid to be pointless', *Herald-Sun*, 26 November 2004.

4   D. Illing, 'Grant chiefs at odds over Nelson veto', *The Australian*, 15 December 2004.

5   G. Healy, 'Axed grants not in national benefit', *Campus Review*, 3 March 2006.

6   ibid.; G. Healy, 'Five ARC grants vetoed', *Campus Review*, 2 February 2005.

7   D. Illing, 'Outsiders get a say in award of grants', *The Australian*, 7 September 2005; Haigh, 'The Nelson touch', p. 26.

8   S. Maiden, 'To put it mildly, critic ready to quit', *The Australian*, 27 September 2005.

9   S. Maiden, 'Nelson begs rebel to stay', *The Australian*, 28 November 2005.

10   D. Illing and M. McKinnon, 'Dust-up down at the ARC', *The Australian*, 29 March 2006.

11   D. Illing, 'Minister vetoes research projects', *The Australian*, 23 November 2005.

12   *Australian Vice-Chancellors' Committee Bulletin*, December 2005; letter from Glyn Davis, chair of the Group of Eight, to the Minister, 21 November 2005; D. Illing, 'Minister's offensive leaves him exposed', *The Australian*, 14 November 2005; S. Morris, 'Veto

alarms academies', *Australian Financial Review*, 14 November 2005; D. Rood, 'Call for change to uni grant process', *The Age*, 16 November 2005; G. Healy, 'Nelson lashed on ARC veto', *Campus Review*, 23 November 2005.

13 D. Illing, 'ARC fear feeds on Nelson's silence', and 'Snitch', *The Australian*, 23 November 2005.

14 Letter from the minister to G. Davis, 21 November 2005.

15 Illing, 'Minister vetoes research projects'; Healy, 'Nelson lashed on ARC veto'.

16 Healy, 'Axed grants not in national benefit'.

17 S. Macintyre, 'Research floored by full Nelson', *The Age*, 16 November 2005; 'Political meddling has become granted', *Sydney Morning Herald*, 16 November 2005.

18 G. Healy, 'Question of Nelson's veto powers over research project grants raised again', *Campus Review*, 16 November 2005.

19 Illing, 'ARC fear feeds on Nelson's silence'.

20 Personal communication.

21 A. Contractor, 'PM overturned uni posting, inquiry told', *Sydney Morning Herald*, 14 August 2001.

22 B. O'Keefe, 'Adult stem-cell bonanza', and L. Drayton, 'Uneasy about centre's funding', *The Australian*, 17 May 2006.

23 Information from a senior member of the University of South Australia.

24 P. Saunders, personal communication.

25 Letter from B. Yates to J. Altman, 7 June 2005; personal communication; Jon Altman, 'Indigenous Affairs Today: The "Influence War" and the attempt to silence the social sciences', Academy of Social Sciences in Australia, Symposium, Canberra, 2005.

26 B. Bessant, 'Robert Gordon Menzies and education in Australia', in *Melbourne Studies in Education 1977*, ed. S. Murray-Smith, Melbourne University Press, Melbourne, 1977, p. 83.

27 Murray Committee, *Report of the Committee on Australian Universities*, Commonwealth Government Printer, Canberra, 1957, pp. 7, 8.

28 ibid., pp. 9, 11.
29 ibid., p. 91.
30 D. Illing, 'Bishop puts faith in peers', *The Australian*, 22 March 2006.
31 <http://www.taxpayer.net/awards/goldenfleece.html>, accessed 31 May 2006.
32 P. Flather, '"Pulling through"—conspiracies, counterplots, and how the SSRC escaped the axe in 1982' in *Social Science Research and Government: Comparative Essays on Britain and the United States*, ed. M. Bulmer, Cambridge University Press, Cambridge, 1987, p. 360.
33 This issue is explored in L. Menand (ed.), *The Future of Academic Freedom*, University of Chicago Press, Chicago, 1996.

4. The research community

1 See <www.unesco.org/science/wcs/eng/framework.htm>.
2 ICSU, 'Standards for Ethics and Responsibility in Science', ISCU, Paris, 2001.
3 Australian Broadcasting Corporation, 'The greenhouse mafia', *Four Corners*, 13 February 2006, <www.abc.net.au/4corners/content/2006/s1566257.htm>.
4 Australian Climate Group, *Climate Change Solutions for Australia*, WWF, Sydney, 2004.
5 AMA/ACF/NCEPH, *Health Impacts of Climate Change*, Australian Medical Association, Canberra, 2005.
6 Australian Business Roundtable on Climate Change, *The Business Case for Early Action*, April 2006, <http://www.businessroundtable.com.au/pdf/F078-RT-WS.pdf>.
7 Australian Broadcasting Corporation, 'The greenhouse mafia'.
8 Personal communication.
9 Australian Broadcasting Corporation, 'The greenhouse mafia'.
10 A. B. Pittock, *Climate Change: Turning up the heat*, CSIRO Publishing, Melbourne, 2005.

11 This section is based on information supplied by Dr Foran, personal communication.

12 A. Wood, 'Narrow views on broadening population', *The Australian*, 5 November 2002.

13 P. Kelly, 'Deep green dilemma', *Weekend Australian*, 9–10 November 2002, p. 28.

14 G. Megalogenis, 'Unleashing the dogma of science', *Weekend Australian*, 9–10 November 2002, p. 4.

15 Department of Education Science and Training, *Australian Science and Technology at a Glance 2005*, <http://www.dest.gov.au/sectors/science_innovation/publications_resources/profiles/australian_science_and_technology_at_a_glance_2005.htm>. See also A. Contractor, 'Growing lag in research spending', *Sydney Morning Herald*, 21 April 2004, <http://www.smh.com.au/articles/2004/04/20/1082395857729.html>.

16 P. Greenfield, personal communication.

17 R. Moynihan, 'It's not easy being green', *Good Weekend Magazine*, 3 September 2005.

18 Katharine Murphy and Sarah Smiles, 'Howard "senses" a nuclear future', *The Age*, 7 June 2006.

19 W. McKibbin, 'Sensible Climate Policy', issues brief, Lowy Institute for International Policy, Sydney, February 2005.

20 G. Pearman, personal communication.

5. Non-government organisations

1 Philanthropy Australia, 'Fact Sheet: The nonprofit sector in Australia', December 2003, <http://www.philanthropy.org.au/factsheets/7-05-03-nonprof.htm>.

2 M. Sawer, 'Governing for the Mainstream: Implications for Community Representation', *Australian Journal of Public Administration*, vol. 61, no. 1, March 2002, pp. 39–49.

3 Organisations that fall into this general category are referred to

variously in the literature as peaks, NGOs, nonprofits, interest groups, charities, community sector organisations and so on. In this chapter the term 'non-government organisations', or NGOs, which is common to the political science literature, will be used.

4 House of Representatives Standing Committee on Community Affairs, 'You have your moments: A report on funding of peak health and community organisations', Australian Government Publishing Service, Canberra, 1991, p. 18.

5 J. Ernst, 'A Competitive Future: the Industry Commission and the Welfare Sector' in *Contesting the Australian Way: States, Markets and Civil Society*, eds B. Cass and P. Smyth, Cambridge University Press, Melbourne, 1998, p. 219.

6 Industry Commission, *Charitable Organisations in Australia*, Report No. 45, Australian Government Publishing Service, Melbourne, 1995, p. 181.

7 RPR cited in Australian Council of Social Services, 'Funding Peak Bodies: ACOSS Response', *ACOSS Info*, no. 218, 2000, pp. 2–3.

8 M. Rawsthorne, 'Government/Non-government partnerships: Towards deliberative democracy in policy making?', a discussion paper for the Western Sydney Community Forum Inc., 2004, p. 4.

9 J. Pixley, 'Social movements, democracy and conflicts over institutional reform' in Cass and Smyth, *Contesting the Australian Way*, p. 143.

10 A. Yeatman, *Activism and the Policy Process*, Allen & Unwin, Sydney, 1998, pp. 3, 17.

11 The Voluntary Sector Initiative, <http://www.vsi-isbc.ca/eng/index.cfm>.

12 National Council for Voluntary Organisations, 'The Compact Between the Government and the Voluntary Sector—the first of its kind in the world', 2001, <http://www.ncvovol.org.uk/Asp/search/ncvo/main.aspx?siteID=1&sID=8&subSID=73&documentID=1216>.

13 D. D'Cruz and G. Johns, 'Green Charities and Partisan Political Campaigning', *IPA Review*, vol. 56, no. 2, June 2004; R. Fox, 'Promoting freedom and community: civil society organisations in Australia', IPA Backgrounder, vol. 18/2, May 2006.

14 J. Staples, 'NGOs out in the cold: the Howard Government policy towards NGOs', Discussion Paper 19/06, June 2006, Democratic Audit of Australia, Canberra.

15 M. Sawer and J. Jupp, 'The two-way street: government shaping of community-based advocacy', *Australian Journal of Public Administration*, vol. 5, no. 54, 1996, p. 84.

16 L. Orchard, 'Public sector reform and the Australian way' in Cass and Smyth, *Contesting the Australian Way*, p. 114.

17 See M. Mowbray, 'Getting NGOs out of the tent: The IPA's campaign against charities', *Harambee*, vol. 13, no. 1, March 2004, <http://www.tear.org.au/resources/harambee/041/04_ngo-out-ofthe-tent.htm>; D'Cruz and Johns, 'Green Charities and Partisan Political Campaigning'.

18 P. Mendes, 'Australian neoliberal think tanks and the backlash against the welfare state', *Journal of Australian Political Economy*, no. 51, June 2003, pp. 29–56; M. Mowbray, 'War on non profits: "NGOs: What do we do about them?"', *Just Policy*, vol. 30, 2003, pp. 3–13.

19 B. Nicholson and G. Hughes, 'Attack on covert project for IPA', *The Age*, 10 August 2003.

20 R. Fox, 'Promoting freedom and community'.

21 J. Howard, 'The Role of Government: A Modern Liberal Approach', The Menzies Research Centre National Lecture Series, Canberra, 6 June 1995.

22 J. Howard, 'Taxation: Keeping faith with Australian families', transcript of the Prime Minister the Hon. John Howard MP, Address to the Menzies Research Centre, Great Hall, Parliament House, Canberra, 18 April 2006, pp. 1–2.

23 G. Pearse, 'The business response to climate change: case studies of Australian interest groups', doctoral thesis, Australian National

University, July 2005; for a discussion see C. Hamilton, 'The Political Economy of Climate Change', The Milthorpe Lecture, Macquarie University, Sydney, 8 June 2006, <http://www.tai. org.au>.

24 G. Pearse, 'The business response to climate change'.

25 Parliamentary Debate, Senate Adjournment: Non-government organisations, 24 June 2004.

26 E. Abetz, 'Electoral reform: making our democracy fairer for all', address to the Sydney Institute, 4 October 2005, <http://www.dofa. gov.au/Media/media_abetz.asp>.

27 S. Maddison, 'Lobbying government' in *Government Communication in Australia*, ed. S. Young, Cambridge University Press, Melbourne, 2007.

28 C. Hamilton and A. Macintosh, *Taming the Panda: The relationship between WWF Australia and the Howard Government*, Discussion Paper No. 68, The Australia Institute, Canberra, 2004.

29 Hamilton and Macintosh, *Taming the Panda*.

30 Reference Group on Welfare Reform, *Participation support for a more equitable society*, July 2000, <http://www.workplace.gov.au/ NR/rdonlyres/97EF2B51-F393-4FCA-AD97-64CCCDFE5258/ 0/McClureReport2000_Final.pdf>.

31 S. Maddison, R. Denniss and C. Hamilton, *Silencing Dissent: non-government organisations and Australian democracy*, Discussion Paper No. 65, The Australia Institute, Canberra, 2004.

32 R. Tomar, 'Redefining NGOs: The emerging debate', *Current Issues Brief*, no. 5, 2003–04, Department of the Parliamentary Library, 2003, p. 4.

33 G. Johns and J. Roskam, *The Protocol: Managing Relations with NGOs*, report to the Prime Minister's Community Business Partnership by the Institute of Public Affairs, 2004, p. 1.

34 S. Maddison, 'Lobbying government'.

35 The Parliament of the Commonwealth of Australia, Charities Bill 2003, p. 5. Exposure draft available at: <http://www.taxboard.gov. au/content/charities_bill_13_june_2003.pdf>.

36 Australian Taxation Office, 'Income tax and fringe benefits tax: charities', draft taxation ruling, 2005, <http://law.ato.gov.au/atolaw/view.htm?docid='DTR/TR2005D6/NAT/ATO/00001/>.

37 S. Peatling, 'Green army warned on politicking', *Sydney Morning Herald*, 12 April 2005.

6. The media

1 Personal communication with the author.

2 Alan Ramsay, 'The Brough and tumble of a cover-up', *Sydney Morning Herald*, 29 July 2006; 'Police raid home of senior Aboriginal public servant', *National Indigenous Times*, no. 110, 27 July 2006.

3 Parliamentary Debate, Senate, Public service amendment regulations 2004: motion for disallowance, 16 June 2005. In 2006 the Minister for Justice and Customs, Senator Ellison, provided official data about the cost of the 'leak squad'. Between 2003 and 2006, 38 cases were investigated by the AFP costing $2 160 940 and utilising 20 980 staff hours. Seven out of the 38 were referred to the CDPP for prosecution.

4 *Lawyer's Weekly*, 'Ruddock goes in to bat for journalists', 11 November 2005, <http://www.lawyersweekly.com.au/articles/86/0C038486.asp?Type=53&Category=853>. On 23 August 2006, the journalists lost an appeal against the contempt charges when the Supreme Court rejected their claim that Victoria's County Court chief judge did not have the power to force them to give pre-trial evidence.

5 L. Oakes, cited in Bryan, 'Gerard McManus and Michael Harvey', filed on *The Oz politics blog* by Bryan on Monday 29 August 2005, <http://www.ozpolitics.info/blog/?p=182>. Confirmed by Oakes in telephone discussion with author, February 2006.

6 Federal Court of Australia, *Bennett v President, Human Rights and Equal Opportunity Commission*, [s003] FCA 1433, December 2003.

7   M. Grattan, 'Gatekeepers and gatecrashers', Deakin Lecture, Melbourne, 2 May 2005.

8   I. Ward, 'The media, power and politics' in *Government, Politics, Power and Policy in Australia*, eds A. Parkin, J. Summers and D. Woodward, Pearson Longman, Sydney, p. 363.

9   The term 'fourth estate' is generally traced to the nineteenth century historian Thomas Carlyle who, in *On Heroes and Hero Worship*, credits Edmund Burke with first describing the media as the fourth estate (or class) of the British Parliament. The other three estates were the clergy, the lords and the 'commoners'.

10 J. Schultz, 'Two cultures: Parliament and the media', Senate Occasional Lecture Series, Parliament House, Canberra, 15 February 2002.

11 J. Schultz, *Reviving the Fourth Estate: Democracy, accountability and the media*, Cambridge University Press, Cambridge, 1998, pp. 5–6.

12 Australian Broadcasting Corporation, *The Role of the National Broadcaster in Contemporary Australia*, Corporate Relations Department, ABC, Sydney, 1985.

13 Schultz, *Reviving the Fourth Estate*, pp. 5–6.

14 M. Simons, 'Inside the ABC' in *Do Not Disturb—Is the Media Failing Australia*, ed. R. Manne, Black Inc., Melbourne, 2005, p. 145.

15 Q. Dempster, 'The slow destruction of the ABC' in R. Manne, *Do Not Disturb*, p. 111.

16 Simons, 'Inside the ABC', pp. 134, 147.

17 Dempster, 'The slow destruction of the ABC', p. 111.

18 H. Ester, unpublished interviews, press gallery, Parliament House, Canberra, 2003–04. This chapter draws on interviews with Geoff Kitney, Michelle Grattan, Glen Milne, Denis Shanahan, Tony Walker, Chris Warren, Rob Chalmers, Louise Dodson, Kerry-Anne Walshe, Richard Griffiths, Jim Middleton, Tony Wright, Malcolm Farr, Ross Peake, Karen Middleton and Alison Carabine.

19 Commonwealth of Australia, *Submission to Senate Inquiry into a Certain Maritime Incident*, Senate Submission No. 13, 15 May 2002.

Final report tabled 23 October 2002. Senate submission available at <http://www.aph.gov.au/senate/committee/maritime_incident_ctte/submissions/sublist.htm>.

20 P. Weller, *Don't Tell the Prime Minister*, Scribe Publications, Melbourne, 2002, pp. 5–6.

7. The public service

1 Australian Public Service, 'Australian Public Service Statistical Bulletin 2004–05', <http://www.apsc.gov.au/stateoftheservice/0405/statistics/table1.htm>.

2 For a detailed listing see P. Williams, 'Howard's legacy: an entrenched, hand-picked elite', *Australian Financial Review*, 16 July 2004, p. 1.

3 Department of Finance document provided to the Senate Finance and Public Administration Committee, 1 November 2005.

4 R. Mulgan, 'Politicising the Australian Public Service?', Research Paper No. 3, 1998–99, Parliament of Australia Library, <http://aph.gov.au/library/pubs/rp/1998-99rp03.htm>.

5 P. Shergold, 'Pride in Public Service', National Press Club Address, Canberra, 15 February 2006.

6 ibid.

7 The Australian Public Service Commission is a public service agency whose role is to 'promote good practice in managing people, support leadership and learning and development in the APS, foster ethical behaviour and workplaces that value diversity'. See <http://www.apsc.gov.auut/introc.htm>.

8 The APSC *State of the Service* report is an annual detailed survey of the APS presented to Parliament. See <http://www.apsc.gov.au/stateoftheservice/0405/index.html>. Figures quoted here are from Chapter 3, Relations with the Government, <http://www.apsc.gov.au/stateoftheservice/0405/c3a.htm>.

9 ibid.

10 Commonwealth of Australia, *APS Values and Code of Conduct in practice: a guide to official conduct for APS employees and agency heads*, Revised edition, Canberra, 2005.

11 R. Garran, 'Admiral to fathom overboard disputes', *The Australian*, 14 November 2001, p. 3.

12 M. Chulov, S. Lewis and P. Karvelas, 'Keelty contradicts PM on Iraq link', *The Australian*, 15 March 2003, p. 4.

13 V. Burgess, 'The power of 10: Howard's decade', *Australian Financial Review*, 1 March 2006, p. 52.

14 See <http://www.apsc.gov.au/stateoftheservice/0405/c3a.htm>.

15 J. Kerr, 'Written-record rule is news to public servants', *The Australian*, 10 March 2006, p. 2.

16 Commonwealth of Australia, 'Senate Select Committee Report on A Certain Maritime Incident', 23 October 2002, <http://www.aph.gov.au/senate/committee/maritime_incident_ctte/index.htm>.

17 D. Marr and M. Wilkinson, *Dark Victory*, Allen & Unwin, Sydney, 2003.

18 Commonwealth of Australia, 'A Certain Maritime Incident', p. xxiii.

19 ibid., p. xiv.

20 ibid., p. xxii.

21 ibid., p. xxiv.

22 ibid., p. xxxiii.

23 ibid., p. xxxiv.

24 ibid., p. 110.

25 S. Maiden, 'Gag in Senate illegal, clerk warns', *The Australian*, 12 April 2006, p. 4; G. Barker, 'Upper house suffers a low blow, clerk warns', *Australian Financial Review*, 12 April 2006, p. 8.

26 Commonwealth of Australia, 'Inquiry into certain Australian companies in relation to the UN Oil-For-Food Programme', <http://www.ag.gov.au//agd/www/UNOilForFoodInquiry.nsf>, Click on Exhibits.

27 For example, on the *PM* program, ABC Radio, 14 March 2006.

28 Commonwealth of Australia, 'Oil-For-Food Inquiry', transcripts,

<http://www.ag.gov.au//agd/www/UNOilForFoodInquiry/Page/Tr anscripts>. See transcript of Innes Willox testimony, 10 April 2006.

29 ibid. See Alexander Downer testimony, 11 April 2006.

30 ibid. See John Howard testimony, 13 April 2006.

31 ibid. See Mark Vaile testimony, 10 April 2006.

32 ibid. See Robert Bowker testimony, 15 Marsh 2006; Jane Drake Brockman testimony, 20 March 2006.

33 L. Briggs, 'Changes in the Australian Public Service', speech to Australian National Audit Office, Canberra, 29 November 2005, <http://www.apsc.gov.au/media/briggs29a1105.htm>.

34 P. Edwards, *Arthur Tange: Last of the Mandarins*, Allen & Unwin, Sydney, 2006, pp. 217–18.

35 ibid., note 37.

36 Briggs, 'Changes in the Australian Public Service', note 36.

37 I. Holland, 'Members of Parliament (Staff) Act: Accountability Issues', Research Note No. 5, 2002–03, Parliament of Australia, Parliamentary Library, <http://www.aph.gov.au/library/pubs/rn/2002-03rn05.htm>.

38 Parliamentary Debate, House of Representatives, 3 March 1994, p. 1713.

39 J. Howard, Garran Oration, Canberra, 19 November 1997, <http://www.pm.gov.au/news/speeches/1997/Garran.html>.

40 Australian Public Service Commission, 'Values in the APS', <http://www.apsc.gov.au/values/index.html>.

41 Australian Public Service Commission, 'APS Code of Conduct', <http://www.apsc.gov.au/conduct/index.html>.

42 Parliamentary Debate, Senate, 14 October 1999, p. 9684.

43 Holland, 'Members of Parliament (Staff) Act: Accountability Issues', note 40.

44 ibid., note 9, p. 25.

45 ibid., note 8.

46 ibid.

47 *Sydney Morning Herald*, 'Press Council upholds complaint over job tender articles', 29 June 2000, p. 8.

48 I. Holland, 'Accountability of Ministerial Staff?', Research Paper No. 19, 2001–02 Parliament of Australia, Parliamentary Library, <http://www.aph.gov.au/library/pubs/rp/2001-02rp19.htm>.

8. Statutory authorities

1 See R. Wettenhall, 'Exploring types of public sector organisations: past exercises and current issues', *Pubic Organization Review*, vol. 3, 2003, pp. 219–45.

2 ibid., p. 232.

3 A. Clark, 'Untold power', *Australian Financial Review*, 23 March 2002.

4 J. Brough, 'Howard to rein in statutory bodies', *Sydney Morning Herald*, 6 March 1997.

5 J. Uhrig, *Review of the Corporate Governance of Statutory Authorities and Office Holders*, Commonwealth of Australia, Canberra, 2003.

6 R. Wettenhall, 'Parliamentary oversight of statutory authorities: A post-Uhrig perspective', *Australasian Parliamentary Review*, vol. 20, no. 2, 2005, p. 41.

7 Ministerial resignations included Peter McGauran, David Jull, Geoff Prosser, Jim Short and Brian Gibson. See A. Macintosh, 'The buck no longer stops with this Government', *Canberra Times*, 19 July 2005; and J. Uhr, 'Ministerial Responsibility in Australia: 2005', paper presented to the Constitutional Law Conference, University of New South Wales, Sydney, 18 February 2005.

8 Brough, 'Howard to rein in statutory bodies'.

9 P. Daley, 'Payback time', *Bulletin*, 21 March 2006. *The Australian* has taken up the Coalition's cause by publishing countless articles on the bias within the ABC, which are similar to articles that have appeared in Murdoch newspapers in the United Kingdom about left-wing bias in the BBC (see K. Inglis, 'Aunty at seventy: A health report on the ABC', *Australian Policy Online*, 27 November 2002).

10 K. Inglis, 'At arms length? The ABC as a Statutory Authority', Australian Fabian Society Autumn Lecture, Assembly Hall, Melbourne, 22 March 2004, <http://www.fabian.org.au/902.asp>.

11 Daley, 'Payback time'.

12 Australian Broadcasting Corporation (ABC), 'Stories in 2002: Michael Kroger and Bias', 2002, <http://www.abc.net.au/media watch/transcripts/130502_s3.htm>.

13 Inglis, 'Aunty at seventy'.

14 R. Ackland, 'The trouble with Kroger's ABC', *The Age*, 11 May 2002.

15 ibid.

16 Over the past decade, Boully has also served on the board of Land and Water Australia, was chair of the Community Advisory Committee of the Murray-Darling Basin Ministerial Council, and was a member of the Australian Heritage Commission and the National River Health Program Advisory Panel.

17 P. Williams, 'Howard's legacy: an entrenched, hand-picked elite', *Australian Financial Review*, 16 July 2004. Mr Newman has held positions on a number of public agencies over the past ten years, including the Financial Sector Advisory Council, the Business Advisory Panel established by the Minister for Multicultural Affairs, and the Year 2000 Steering Committee.

18 R. Brunton, 'Controversy in the Sickness Country: The Battle Over Coronation Hill', *Quadrant*, September 1991; and R. Brunton, 'Mining Credibility: Coronation Hill and the anthropologists', *Anthropology Today*, vol. 8, no. 2, 1992.

19 P. Wolfe, 'Indigenous commentator needs to substantiate latest claim', *The Australian*, 24 May 1997.

20 R. Brunton, *Black Suffering, White Guilt? Aboriginal disadvantage and the Royal Commission into Aboriginal Deaths in Custody*, Institute of Public Affairs, 1993.

21 R. Brunton, 'Rights and Recompense in Australia', *Wall Street Journal Asia*, 31 August 1993.

22 R. Brunton, *Betraying the Victim: The Stolen Generations Report*, Institute of Public Affairs, Melbourne, 1998. For discussion of Brunton's paper see H. Wootten, 'Ron Brunton and *Bringing Them Home*', *Indigenous Law Bulletin*, vol. 4, no. 12, 1998. See also R. Brunton, 'White and Black: Why bother with facts?', *Review*, Institute of Public Affairs, vol. 50, no. 4, 1998; and R. Brunton, 'Genocide, the "Stolen Generations", and the "Unconceived Generations"', *Quadrant*, vol. 42, no. 5, 1998.

23 See R. Brunton, 'The divide of Hindmarsh', *Courier-Mail*, 14 February 1994; R. Brunton, *Blocking Business: An Anthropological Assessment of the Hindmarsh Island Dispute*, Occasional Paper No. B31, Tasman Institute, August 1995; and R. Brunton, 'Hindmarsh Island and the hoaxing of Australian anthropology', *Quadrant*, vol. 43, no. 5, 1999, pp. 11–17. See also M. Simons, 'Hindmarsh: where lies the truth?', *The Age*, 9 May 2003.

24 Brunton, 'The divide of Hindmarsh'.

25 Brunton, 'Traditions that trap', *The Australian*, 16 November 1996.

26 See *Chapman v Luminis Pty Ltd (No. 5)*, FCA 1106, 2001. For further details on the affair see M. Simons, *The Meeting of the Waters: The Hindmarsh Island Affair*, Hodder Headline, Australia, 2003.

27 Daley, 'Payback time'.

28 K. Windschuttle, 'The return of postmodernism in Aboriginal history', *Quadrant*, vol. 50, no. 4, April 2006.

29 K. Windschuttle, *Unemployment: A social and political analysis of the economic crisis in Australia*, Pelican Books, Australia, 1980.

30 L. Murray, 'New ABC director, same old problem', *Sydney Morning Herald*, 17–18 June 2006.

31 See M. Rucci, 'We were as popular as dandruff', *The Advertiser*, 6 May 2006; and Murray, 'New ABC director, same old problem'.

32 P. Hurley, 'Wrong to call me a powerbroker', *The Advertiser*, 11 May 2006.

33 Daley, 'Payback time'.

34 ABC, 'Meet the ABC's new managing director: Mark Scott', 2006,

<http://www.abc.net.au/rn/mediareport/stories/2006/1646075. htm>; and ABC, 'ALP praises ABC chief's media background', 2006, <http://www.abc.net.au/am/content/2006/s1644039.htm>.

35 P. McGuinness, 'New ABC Tory chief won't rock the boat', *The Australian*, 23 May 2006.

36 See ABC, 'ALP praises ABC chief's media background'.

37 ibid.

38 A. Ramsay, 'Our ABC is Under Siege', *Sydney Morning Herald*, 12 June 1996.

39 L. Tanner, 'How to stop the stacking of the ABC board', *The Age*, 25 April 2003.

40 See Senate Environment, Communications, Information Technology and the Arts References Committee, *Above Board? Methods of Appointment to the ABC Board*, Commonwealth of Australia, Canberra, 2001, p. 11.

41 Past governments had taken steps to limit the commission's autonomy before it was abolished. However, by making the council an advisory body, the government has ensured the council has very little independence.

42 There are now four main federal heritage lists: the list of World Heritage areas (places of international significance); the National Heritage List (places of national significance); the Commonwealth Heritage List (places of significance on Commonwealth land or in Commonwealth waters); and the Register of the National Estate (any site of heritage significance).

43 At the time of writing, there were 29 places on the list. Only one of these sites was listed as a natural heritage site and only five sites were listed as having Indigenous heritage values. Two of the five sites of Indigenous significance were listed because they were the site of early interaction between Europeans and Indigenous Australians and they commemorated other aspects of Australia's colonial history. The three other Indigenous sites were only listed because they are of archaeological importance—not because of their importance to the relevant Indigenous communities.

44 For example, the minister did not comply with the statutory requirements in relation to the decisions regarding the Aboriginal Tent Embassy and Old Parliament House in Canberra.

45 I. Campbell, Proof Committee Hansard—Senate, Environment, Communications, Information Technology and the Arts Legislation Committee, Commonwealth of Australia, 25 May 2006, p. 116.

46 ABC, 'Thomson explains absence', 2001, <http://www.abc.net.au/pm/stories/s328220.htm>.

47 For example, Barrow Island and the Burrup Peninsula in Western Australia and the Wara-Nhayara Plateau in New South Wales were nominated for inclusion on the National Heritage List, and BHP has a financial interest in all three sites. Mr Harley disclosed the company's interest in these sites, but according to government documents he did not excuse himself from the council's deliberations concerning their suitability for listing.

48 See H. Forbes-Mewett, G. Griffin and D. McKenzie, 'The Australian Industrial Relations Commission: Adapting or dying?', *International Journal of Employment Studies*, vol. 11, no. 2, 2003, pp. 1–24.

49 Williams, 'Howard's legacy'.

50 K. Murphy, 'Jobs advocate attacks Labor's IR policy', *Australian Financial Review*, 2 April 2001.

51 ibid.

52 See P. Reith, 'New Head for OEA', Media Release, 1998, <http://mediacentre.dewr.gov.au/mediacentre/AllReleases/1998/December/NewHeadForOea.htm>; and Office of the Employment Advocate, *The Advocate*, OEA newsletter, no. 20, 2004, Commonwealth of Australia, Canberra.

53 A. Horin, 'A moral duty: maintain the wage', *Sydney Morning Herald*, 1 April 2006.

54 ibid.

55 I. Harper and S. Gregg, 'Forgive us our debts? Jubilee 2000: The unanswered questions', *Issue Analysis*, no. 8, 28 September 1999.

56 I. Harper, 'Quo Vadis Australia?', *Policy*, vol. 18, no. 1, 2002, pp. 46–50.

57 See Australian Broadcasting Corporation, 'New Light Shed on New Fair Pay Commission Head', 2005, <http://www.abc.net.au/pm/content/2005/s1532116.htm>; and Australian Broadcasting Corporation, 'Business dealings of wage chief questioned', 2005, <http://www.abc.net.au/am/content/2005/s1535473.htm>.

58 Horin, 'A moral duty: maintain the wage'.

59 MiniMovers, 'About MiniMovers', 2006, <http://www.mmjobs.com.au/mmjobs/about/>.

60 See Office of the Employment Advocate, *Annual Report 2004/05*, Commonwealth of Australia, Canberra, 2005; and Office of the Employment Advocate, *The Advocate*, OEA newsletter, issues 27 and 28, 2005.

61 ibid.

62 ibid.; and P. McIlwain, 'The truth about Australian workplace agreements', 2005, <http://www.oea.gov.au/graphics.asp?showdoc=/news/2005/letterstatement_050715.asp>.

63 See P. Switzer, 'Warning on award system penalties', *The Australian*, 28 June 2005; P. Switzer, 'They're MiniMovers and shakers', *The Australian*, 5 July 2005; S. Dziedzic, 'One of Howard's new movers and shakers', *The Australian*, 13 July 2005; S. Balogh, 'Workforce on move to AWAs', *Courier-Mail*, 30 June 2004; and L. Molina, 'Focus on workplace deals', *Courier-Mail*, 20 July 2005.

64 See Office of the Employment Advocate, *The Advocate*, OEA newsletter, issue 20, 2004.

65 K. Andrews, 'Establishment of the Office of Workplace Services as an independent agency', media release, Commonwealth of Australia, Canberra, 30 March 2006.

66 See A. Macintosh, 'Industrial relations "watchdog" is a lapdog', *Canberra Times*, 28 July 2006.

67 See *National Museum of Australia Act 1980*, Section 6.

68 Pearson is now a conservative columnist for *The Australian*. In

2003, he was appointed to the board of SBS, where he joined Liberal Party member and former editor in chief of *The West Australian* Bob Cronin, and Carla Zampatti, whose husband, John Spender, is a former Liberal MP.

69 National Museum of Australia, *Annual Report 2001–2002*, Commonwealth of Australia, Canberra, 2002, p. v.

70 C. Kremmer, 'Casualty of the history wars', *Sydney Morning Herald*, 6 December 2003.

71 K. Windschuttle, 'How not to run a museum: people's history at the post-modern museum', *Quadrant*, vol. 45, no. 9, September 2001.

72 Windschuttle, 'How not to run a museum'.

73 M. Devine, 'Museum sneers at white history of Australia', *Daily Telegraph*, 12 March 2001.

74 See Windschuttle, 'How not to run a museum'; and G. McCarthy, 'The "new" cultural wars: "constructing" the National Museum of Australia', paper presented to the Australasian Political Studies Association Conference, University of Adelaide, Adelaide, 29 September to 1 October 2004.

75 G. Davison, 'Exhibiting a revisionist view of our history', *The Age*, 12 December 2002.

76 C. Kremmer, 'Dawn breaks at hand of right, who see museum as mistake by the lake', *Sydney Morning Herald*, 6 December 2003.

77 Kremmer, 'Casualty of the history wars'; McCarthy, 'The "new" cultural wars'; and K. Lundy, 'Interference in the National Museum puts Australian culture under seige', *On Line Opinion*, 5 December 2003, <http://www.onlineopinion.com.au>.

78 Simons, 'Hindmarsh: where lies the truth?'.

79 J. Carroll, R. Longes, P. Jones and P. Vickers-Rich, *Review of the National Museum of Australia, Its Exhibitions and Public Programs: A Report to the Council of the National Museum of Australia*, Commonwealth of Australia, Canberra, 2003.

80 Williams, 'Howard's legacy'.

9. The military and intelligence services

1 Commonwealth of Australia, *APS Values and Code of Conduct in Practice: A guide to official conduct for APS employees and agency heads*, Revised edition, 2005, Chapter 2, <http://www.apsc.gov.au/values/conductguidelines4.htm>.

2 Varghese and O'Sullivan filled the role of senior adviser (international) on Howard's staff prior to taking up their appointments as director-general of ONA and director-general of security.

3 That McNarn is unlikely to cause the government any angst was my personal observation during some twenty years' service in the Defence Force, during which time I reached the rank of Lieutenant Colonel and associated with colleagues and subordinates of McNarn.

4 D. Richardson, appearing as a witness at the Parliamentary Joint Committee on ASIO, ASIS and DSD, Parliament House, Canberra, 19 May 2005.

5 P. Varghese, appearing as a witness at the Senate Finance and Public Administration References and Legislation Committee, Parliament House, Canberra, 13 February 2006.

6 That the security-vetting process has been tightened in recent years is the observation of former and serving intelligence officials with whom I have had contact.

7 Specifically Section 16, 'Protection for whistleblowers', of the *Public Service Act 1999*.

8 Specifically Section 37, 'Protection from civil actions', of the *Ombudsman Act 1976*.

9 Specifically Section 70, 'Disclosure of information by Commonwealth officers', of the *Crimes Act 1914*.

10 Specifically Division 91, 'Offences relating to espionage and similar activities', of the *Criminal Code Act 1995*.

11 For instance Section 79, 'Official secrets', of the *Crimes Act 1914*, which specifies two years imprisonment for knowingly communicating protected official information.

12 *Criminal Code Amendment (Espionage and Related Matters) Act 2002.*

13 Senate Hansard, 3 August 2004, pp. 25, 533.

14 ibid.

15 M. Scrafton, appearing as a witness at the Senate Select Committee on the Scrafton Evidence, Parliament House, Canberra, 1 September 2004.

16 N. Minchin and H. Coonan, 'Proposal to Reform the Senate Committee System', joint media release, 20 June 2006.

17 K. Burton, *Scrutiny or secrecy? Committee oversight of foreign and national security policy in the Australian Parliament*, Parliamentary Library, Canberra, 2004, pp. 15–16.

18 J. Howard, quoted in C. Banham, 'Howard agrees to show Labor secret spy report', *Sydney Morning Herald*, 24 July 2004.

19 R. Hill, media conference, Sydney, 14 December 2004.

20 Lewincamp was granted the Public Service Medal on 26 January 2004 for 'outstanding public service in the provision of high quality intelligence for the strategic planning and conduct of the Australian contribution to the Iraq War'. See <http://www.itsanhonour.gov.au/honours/honour_roll/search.cfm?aus_award_id=1056499&search_type=quick&showInd=true>.

21 Farmer was made an Officer of the Order of Australia on 13 June 2005 for 'service to the community through contributions to Australias [sic] international relations and to major public policy development including domestic security, border systems, immigration, multicultural affairs and Indigenous service delivery'. See <http://www.itsanhonour.gov.au/honours/honour_roll/search.cfm?aus_award_id=1058525&search_type=quick&showInd=true>.

22 Commonwealth of Australia, *Report of the Inquiry into the Circumstances of the Immigration Detention of Cornelia Rau*, Canberra, July 2005.

23 For example, A. Downer, interviewed by K. Gilbert, *Sky News*, 3 February 2006.

24 As reported by C. McGrath, ABC Radio National, *PM*, 27 April 2006.

25 Parliamentary Joint Committee on ASIO, ASIS and DSD, *Intelligence on Iraq's weapons of mass destruction*, Parliament of Australia, Canberra, December 2003.

26 P. Flood, *Report of the Inquiry into the Australian Intelligence Agencies*, Canberra, July 2004.

27 Attorney-General's Department, Inquiry into certain Australian companies in relation to the UN Oil-for-Food Program, *Terms of Reference*, 10 November 2005, and *Revised Terms of Reference*, 6 February, 10 and 17 March 2006, <http://www.ag.gov.au/agd/www/UNoilforfoodinquiry.nsf/Page/Terms_of_Reference>.

28 ABC Online, 'Nelson's Kovco comments "not part of investigation"', 1 June 2006, <http://www.abc.net.au/news/newsitems/200606/s1652758.htm>.

29 This information was provided by a reliable source on his return from service in Iraq.

30 A relatively new addition to the better literature on the politics of fear is provided by C. Lawrence, *Fear and Politics*, Scribe, Melbourne, 2006.

31 A. Dupont and G. Pearman, *Heating Up the Planet: Climate change and security*, Lowy Institute Paper No. 12, Lowy Institute for International Policy, Sydney, 2006.

32 Parliamentary Joint Committee on ASIO, ASIS and DSD, *Intelligence on Iraq's weapons of mass destruction*, p. 94; and P. Flood, *Report of the Inquiry into the Australian Intelligence Agencies*, p. 25.

33 Parliamentary Joint Committee on ASIO, ASIS and DSD, *Intelligence on Iraq's weapons of mass destruction*, p. 93.

34 A.O. Hirschman, *Exit, Voice, and Loyalty: Responses to Decline in Firms, Organizations, and States*, Harvard University Press, Cambridge, 1970.

35 ibid., p. 78.

36 Lord Hutton, *Report of the Inquiry into the Circumstances Surrounding the Death of Dr David Kelly*, The Hutton Inquiry, London, 28 January 2004.

37 ABC, 'Intelligence Wars: Behind the Lance Collins Affair', *Background Briefing*, ABC Radio National, 30 May 2004; ABC, 'Burnt by the Sun', *Australian Story*, ABC Television, 25 July 2005; L. Collins and W. Reed, *Plunging Point: Intelligence failures, cover-ups and consequences*, Fourth Estate, Sydney, 2005.

38 Letters to the Editor, *The Australian*, 16 August 2004.

39 Scrafton, appearing as a witness at the Senate Select Committee on the Scrafton Evidence Report, Canberra, 9 December 2004.

40 ABC, 'Secrets and Lies', *Four Corners*, ABC Television, 14 February 2005; R. Barton, *The Weapons Detective: The inside story of Australia's top weapons inspector*, Black Inc., Melbourne, 2006.

41 SBS Online, 'Government does not pressure intelligence agencies: Howard', 14 April 2004, <http://www9.sbs.com.au/theworldnews/region.php?id=82989&region=7>.

42 ABC, 'Burnt by the Sun'.

43 *Report of the Senate Select Committee on the Scrafton Evidence*, Parliament of Australia, Canberra, December 2004, pp. 57, 74.

44 H. McDonald, 'Words of Mass Deception', *Sydney Morning Herald*, 13 May 2006.

45 J. Howard, House of Representatives, Canberra, 17 February 2005.

46 It should be said that Kate is a former colleague and now my partner.

47 Parliamentary Joint Committee on ASIO, ASIS and DSD, *Intelligence on Iraq's weapons of mass destruction*, pp. 107–8.

48 This information came to my attention when I was invited to fill the vacancy at the event.

49 The senior strategic analyst involved with Iraq is still in government service and should remain nameless. The information regarding Ungerer was provided by him in an unpublished statement.

50 ABC, 'Labor claims defence force politicised', *The World Today*, ABC Radio National, 13 October 2003, <http://www.abc.net.au/worldtoday/content/2005/s1481408.htm>.

51 C. Fernandes, *Reluctant Saviour*, Scribe, Melbourne, 2004.

52 A. Bolt, 'Spook misspoke', *Herald-Sun*, 23 June 2003.

53 A. Wilkie, *Axis of Deceit*, Black Inc., Melbourne, 2004.

54 The specific text cannot be identified because of the terms of a Deed of Agreement insisted upon by the government during the censorship process.

55 In 2002 US Federal Bureau of Investigation (FBI) whistleblower Coleen Rowley revealed that FBI Headquarters in Washington had failed to understand and act on information provided by FBI officers before 9/11 about the so-called 20th hijacker, Zacarias Moussaoui. An edited version of the memo to FBI Director Robert Mueller that first signalled her concern can be found at: <http://www.time.com/time/covers/1101020603/memo.html>.

56 Details of the accountability regime for the intelligence agencies can be found at: <http://www.igis.gov.au/account.cfm>.

10. The Senate

1 H. Coonan, 'The Senate: Safeguard or Handbrake on Democracy?', address to the Sydney Institute, 3 February 2003; Department of the Prime Minister and Cabinet, *Resolving Deadlocks: A Discussion Paper on Section 57 of the Constitution*, Canberra, 2003.

2 For such classic notions, see J. Uhr, *Deliberative Democracy in Australia: The Changing Place of Parliament*, Cambridge University Press, Cambridge, 1998, and the authorities cited at pp. 63–6, 70–4.

3 This exchange is in correspondence and advices attached to the report of the committee, *Matters Relating to the Gallipoli Peninsula*, October 2005.

4 *Combet v Commonwealth* [2005] HCA 61, reasons for judgment, 21 October 2005, at 89.

5 ibid., at 27.

6 ibid., at 7.

7 Senate Debates, 7 September 2005, pp. 104–24.

11. Signs of resistance

1 Parliamentary Debate, House of Representatives, Migration Amendment (Designated Unauthorised Arrivals) Bill 2006, 9 August.

2 ibid.

3 M. Wilkinson, 'Weapons cover-up revealed', *Sydney Morning Herald*, 31 August 2006.

4 Australian Broadcasting Corporation, 'Major charities believe new welfare rules are unfair', *The World Today*, ABC Radio, 30 June 2006, <http://www.abc.net.au/worldtoday/content/2006/s1675 802.htm>.

5 Catholic News, 'New welfare-to-work rules spell disaster: Catholic Social Services', 3 July 2006, <http://www.cathnews.com/news/ 607/3.php>.

6 Australian Broadcasting Corporation, 'Defence Force Chief criticises Brendan Nelson in statement to Kovko inquiry', *The World Today*, ABC Radio, 8 September 2006, <http://www.abc.net.au/ worldtoday/content/2006/s1736261.htm>.

INDEX

An 'n' after a page number indicates that the reference is to an endnote.

Growth Fetish

Clive Hamilton

ISBN 978 1 74114 078 1

For decades our political leaders and opinion makers have touted higher incomes as the way to a better future. Economic growth means better lives for us all. But after many years of sustained economic growth and increased personal incomes we must confront an awful fact: we aren't any happier. This is the great contradiction of modern politics.

In this provocative book, Clive Hamilton argues that, far from being the answer to our problems, growth fetishism and the marketing society lie at the heart of our social ills. They have corrupted our social priorities and political structures, and have created a profound sense of alienation among young and old.

Growth Fetish is the first serious attempt at a politics of change for rich countries dominated by the sicknesses of affluence, where the real yearning is not for more money but for authentic identity, and where the future lies in a new relationship with the natural environment.

'Right on target, and badly needed.'—**Noam Chomsky**

'Clive Hamilton's garbage is just silly, dangerous, left-wing crap.'—**Michael Egan, NSW Treasurer**

'Australia's most amazing economist . . . You will find [*Growth Fetish*] either exhilarating or deeply threatening.'—**Ross Gittens,** *Sydney Morning Herald*

Affluenza
When too much is never enough

Clive Hamilton with Richard Denniss

ISBN 978 1 74114 671 4

Our houses are bigger than ever, but our families are smaller. Our kids go to the best schools we can afford, but we hardly see them. We've got more money to spend, yet we're further in debt than ever before. What is going on?

The Western world is in the grip of a consumption binge that is unique in human history. We aspire to the lifestyles of the rich and famous at the cost of family, friends and personal fulfilment. Rates of stress, depression and obesity are up as we wrestle with the emptiness and endless disappointments of the consumer life.

Affluenza pulls no punches, claiming our whole society is addicted to overconsumption. It tracks how much Australians overwork, the growing mountains of stuff we throw out, the drugs we take to 'self-medicate' and the real meaning of 'choice'. Fortunately there is a cure. More and more Australians are deciding to ignore the advertisers, reduce their consumer spending and recapture their time for the things that really matter.

'Clive Hamilton and Richard Denniss ... set out on paths others don't go down, then explore without fear or favour and finally draw conclusions about modern Australia, warts and all. It's all accompanied by passion which is why the results cannot be ignored.' —**Geraldine Doogue, ABC broadcaster**

'Fascinating—at the same time a call to arms and a chill-pill, *Affluenza* challenges not just individuals, but society itself.'—**Adam Spencer, comedian, mathematician and ABC broadcaster**

'*Affluenza* is a lively read with a punishingly compelling tone.'—*The Age*

'(*Affluenza*) high-lights in a readable, fast-paced way the centrally important issue of overconsumption . . .'—*Arena Magazine*